ACKNOWLEDGMENTS

First and most importantly, I'd like to express deep thanks to my wife, Michelle, for her constant support and encouragement. I couldn't do it without you, babe.

Thanks to Josh Moshier for lending his arranging talents to this project. Thanks to Andrew Haynie for donating his saxophone skills to the "All Blues" recording. Thanks to Colin Oldberg, Jean Laurenz, and Paul Floreck for your professionalism, your chops, and your friendship. Also, a big thanks to Kurt Plahna, whose editorial advice and expertise has been indispensable.

I'd also like to express profound gratitude to all my teachers and students who have inspired and challenged me, and given me the opportunity to grow as a teacher, student, musician, and human being. Education is our most precious resource. Thank your teachers!

This book is dedicated to my parents, Andrea and Dave, and to my other parents, Gwen and Curly. Your support and encouragement are priceless.

BRIEF CONTENTS

FULL CONTENTS

9
10–12

INTRODUCTION

Say all you have to say in the fewest possible words, or your reader will be sure to skip them; and in the plainest possible words or you will certainly be misunderstood.

—John Ruskin (1819–1900)

What's Ahead:
- Book overview
- Chapter overview
- How to use the book

Hi, and welcome to *All About Trumpet!* If you're new to trumpet playing, this book will get you started and help instill good learning habits. If you already play or are a teacher, this book may give you new insight and information. The goal of this book is to help you along in your journey toward mastery of the trumpet and to give you the necessary resources to achieve your goals. Once you've absorbed this book, you'll have a great foundation from which to build a lifetime of playing music on your trumpet. That's the whole point, right?

This book will help ease you into the world of playing trumpet with the knowledge and tricks I've learned from over 25 years of playing and more than 15 years of teaching. You'll start with the most basic ideas and build on them until you've learned about the trumpet from end to end, inside and out.

ABOUT THE BOOK

All About Trumpet will take you through almost everything you need to play trumpet, including how to get a sound, how to breathe, how to increase your range and endurance, how to clean your instrument, and much more. All this information is shown to you in small doses so you won't feel overwhelmed by all that needs to be learned. Chapters are short and easy to get through, though mastering the information they contain will continue long after the chapter has been read.

That's a good thing. This book is meant to be a reference, which means you *will* come back to it again and again on your journey towards trumpet mastery. Reading the book one time through will certainly increase your understanding, but you'll have to spend some time with these concepts to make them truly stick and become a part of your musicianship. Come back to the book from time to time for a review, and get some help from a good teacher.

All About Trumpet deals with specific aspects of playing the trumpet and not much time is spent on the skills of reading music. Basic concepts will be explained, but for more specific information on reading music, check out *Basic Music Theory: How to Read, Write, and Understand Written Music.* You can find it at www.sol-ut.com (including free samples of the book).

THE LAYOUT OF THE BOOK

The book is organized into four major sections, which are further broken up into chapters. Here's a quick rundown of what to expect from each.

Section 1: The Bare Necessities

This section covers everything you need to get a sound on the horn, including how to find one, what to look for in a mouthpiece, making the lip buzz, and how to practice.

Section 2: Getting into It

In this section, you're going to start to learn about musical notation and many other basic concepts, like breathing, tonguing, lip slurs, range, and endurance. After all that practicing, you might notice that your horn has grown some gunk in it, and this section will also help you take your horn apart for a thorough cleaning.

Section 3: Tricks and Treats

This section explores other aspects of playing trumpet, like cool sound effects you can get on your horn, discographies of great trumpet music, mutes to stick in your horn, gear to help make playing more fun and rewarding, and trumpet luminaries who have shown us what the trumpet is capable of.

Section 4: Jammin' with the Pros

In this section you get to study five full-length transcriptions of popular songs from musicians such as Miles Davis, the Beatles, Thelonious Monk, Tito Puente, and more. Some of the recordings have just rhythm section so you can begin to improvise, which is one of the most fun things musicians do.

Appendix: This is an appendix you won't have to remove surgically. In here you'll find supplemental material, like a track list and fingering chart.

Do I Need to Read Music? At first, no. In fact, once you've got a good buzz, you should avoid written music altogether and simply experiment with the horn. This will prepare you for eventually reading music. And if reading isn't something you're interested in, the audio CD (and fingerings) will allow you to play by ear. *All About Trumpet* deals with specific aspects of playing the trumpet and only a little space is devoted to the valuable skill of reading music. Basic concepts of written music will be explained, but for more specific information on reading music, check out *Basic Music Theory: How to Read, Write, and Understand Written Music* at www.sol-ut.com. Reading music is a great tool, but not absolutely necessary. It's more important that you enjoy playing.

ABOUT THE CD

Follow the audio icons in the book (see page 4 for Icon Legend) to keep your spot on the CD. The track icons are placed at the top of each musical figure. Included are samples of basic techniques such as buzzing and tonguing as well as more challenging techniques. Also included are short excerpts of tunes in many styles from classical, to rock, to jazz.

As you go through this book, the CD should help make you a better trumpet player. Some of the musical examples are challenging to read, so the CD should help you through those tough ones. The CD should not be used as a substitute for learning to read music. Listening and reading should go together. Occasionally, supplemental recorded and written material for this book can be found at www.sol-ut.com.

The Players

Jonathan Harnum, Trumpet: Harnum has a master's degree in music education from Northwestern University and is currently a PhD student in music education at Northwestern University. Jon has played trumpet for over 25 years in many different styles with many musicians, has been an active, in-demand teacher for over 15 years, and is the author of the popular book *Basic Music Theory: How to Read, Write, and Understand Written Music*. More information can be found at www.sol-ut.com.

George Fludas, Drums: Fludas is a Chicago-based jazz drummer who can be heard frequently in Chicago at the Jazz Showcase, the Green Mill, and Pete Miller's. He often works with the Ron Perrillo trio and the Chicago Jazz Orchestra. He was a member of Ray Brown's trio in 2000-2001 and has performed with many jazz greats, such as Clark Terry, Johnny Griffin, Cedar Walton, Hank Jones, Tommy Flanagan, Frank Wess, Bobby Hutcherson, Eric Alexander, and Diana Krall.

Dennis Carroll, Bass: Dennis is a member of both the Bobby Broom Trio and the Ron Perrillo Trio and has also performed with Benny Golson, Ron Blake, Slide Hampton, Eric Alexander, Frank Wess, George Coleman, Roy Hargrove, James Moody, Charles McPherson, and Bobby Hutcherson. Carroll has recorded with Bobby Broom, Jodi Christian, Von Freeman, Ira Sullivan, Lin Halliday, and Clark Terry (with the Chicago Jazz Orchestra), and he has performed extensively throughout the world at venues such as the Chicago Jazz Festival, the Estoril Jazz Festival in Portugal, the Knitting Factory in New York City, the Kennedy Center Awards, and Symphony Center in Chicago.

Seán McCluskey, Piano/Keys: Seán McCluskey is a professional pianist and music educator living in Chicago. He received his bachelor of music degree from Northwestern University, where he majored in Jazz Studies. At sixteen, he was one three pianists and seventeen musicians selected nationally to attend the Dave Brubeck Institute Summer Jazz Colony on full scholarship. While at Northwestern he had the opportunity to study classical piano with Karen Kan-Walsh, and jazz piano with Michael Kocour and Joan Hickey. Seán has performed with such jazz notables as David Liebman, Maria Schneider, Christian McBride, Bob Mintzer, Joel Spencer, and Bobby Broom, and has also performed solo classical piano at the Kennedy Center in Washington D.C.

Colin Oldberg, Jean Laurenz, and Paul Floreck are majoring in Classical Trumpet Performance at Northwestern University. Jean is pursuing a double major in music education with a choral emphasis.

Recorded at Studiomedia in Evanston, Illinois

Mastered at Studiomedia by Andrew Arbetter

ICON LEGEND

Included in every *All About* book are several icons to help you on your way. Keep an eye out for these.

AUDIO

This icon indicates a related track on the accompanying CD.

TRY THIS

Included with this icon are various bits of helpful advice about trumpet playing.

EXTRAS

This includes additional information on various topics that may be interesting and useful, but not necessarily essential.

DON'T FORGET

There's a lot of information in this book that may be difficult to remember. This refresher will help you stay the course.

DANGER!

Here, you'll learn how to avoid injury and keep your equipment from going on the fritz.

NUTS & BOLTS

Included with this last icon are tidbits on the fundamentals or building blocks of music.

SECTION **1**

The Bare Necessities

CHAPTER 1

FINDING A 'PIECE OF THE ACTION

There is nothing more notable in Socrates than that he found time, when he was an old man, to learn music and dancing, and thought it time well spent.

—Michel de Montaigne (1533–1592)

What's Ahead:
- How to find a good instrument
- Mouthpiece essentials
- How to find the right mouthpiece
- Mouthpiece size chart

GOT HORN?

You probably already have a trumpet or cornet, and if so, you still might want to read this section to be sure you've got a horn that's going to work well for you. Also, we trumpet players usually like to have many instruments (and even more mouthpieces!), so you can use this brief guide to help you when you buy your second horn.

Parts of the Trumpet You Should Know

When buying a horn, I've given you advice below about the valves, the lead pipe, and a couple other things. So you know what I'm talking about, here are the basic parts of the trumpet:

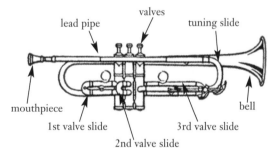

Consider Renting or Leasing

Most music stores will rent you an instrument, and many will put your rental fee towards the purchase of the instrument if you decide to stick with it. You can either rent a brand new instrument or, for a lesser fee, rent a used instrument. If you rent to own you may end up paying a little more than purchasing an instrument outright, but this is a good option if you're not sure you'll stick with this instrument or if you have limited savings to spend.

Where to Look

The end of a school year is a good time to look for a horn. This is often a time when instruments become available from those who have decided to discontinue their studies. Your local music store is also a good source of instruments for sale and information.

You don't have to buy a trumpet new from a music store. There are several alternatives available to you and with many of them you'll save some cash. Following is a list of some options along with pros and cons about the choice.

- Ask Around: Ask friends and relatives if anyone has a trumpet in an attic or basement that's not being used. Thousands and thousands of horns are bought every year and many of them go unused. They're out there, and someone you know might have one. If that someone is a good friend or a relative, you might get the trumpet for free or be able to borrow it.

- Garage Sales: **PRO**: the absolute cheapest way to find an instrument. **CON**: It's not often you'll find a trumpet at a garage sale, but try calling first if you have a number. Take a trumpet player with you. Be sure to test out any horn you find (more on this below). **TIP**: Ask someone you know who visits garage sales regularly to keep an eye out for a trumpet for you. Be sure to offer less than the seller is asking unless what they're offering is too good to be true. If this is the case, be careful, it may be too good to be true.

- Classified Ads: **PRO**: This can be one of the least expensive options for finding a horn. It's easy as long as you can read and have a local paper. **CON**: Hit and miss. It's no guarantee you'll find a trumpet here (especially if you live in a small town), and if you do, you'll have to go find it and test it out. **TIP**: Take a trumpet player with you. Ask the seller to come down on the price, no matter what it is. Because they placed an ad, they're eager to sell and probably are asking more than they would actually take.

- Pawn Shop: **PRO**: also often an inexpensive option. A phone call can determine whether a pawn shop has a trumpet. **CON**: As above, no guarantees that a pawn shop will have a trumpet. It may be in poor condition (though this can be a benefit to you if it only needs minor repair or simple cleaning). If you find one, be sure to test it before you buy. **TIP**: Take a trumpet player with you. Ask the seller to come down on the price, no matter what it is. A pawn shop will ask more for a horn than they'll probably take. Beware that most pawn shop owners are very good at haggling.

- E-Bay (www.ebay.com): **PRO**: E-Bay always has many trumpets listed both from professional companies and individuals. Do your homework so you know what you want because you'll probably find it. The bidding system is often a good way to get an instrument a little cheaper, but this can also backfire and you could pay more than a horn is worth. Run a search on the horn you're interested in to find what prices are reasonable. **CON**: You can't try out the horn or be sure it is all the seller says it is. Though it's rare, some people have been ripped off by bogus offers. **TIP**: Check the seller's rating to see if they have sold on E-Bay before (the more positive ratings the better, of course), and if possible, correspond with the seller via e-mail or phone and ask questions about the instrument. Ask the seller to play the horn over the phone. Don't pay the entire amount for the instrument up front. Pay half and send the other half when you receive (and check out) the horn. This may require an additional agreement with the seller.

- Craig's List (http://chicago.craigslist.org/about/cities.html): **PRO**: If you live in or near a large urban city, you can find people selling trumpets. You might find a good instrument at a fair price in this way. As with the E-Bay option, do your homework about a horn, ask for pictures, and ask to play the horn before you buy it. **CON**: These transactions are private, and there are no guarantees or protections offered by larger companies like E-Bay, Pay-Pal, etc. **TIP**: I've bought things, sold a few, and found an apartment through Craig's list and had good experiences. People are usually honest. Be sure to ask questions about the horn and try to set up an appointment to play it.

Don't give up. Ask around and visit or call garage sales and you'll find a horn waiting for you eventually. It might be easiest at the music store, where you're sure to get a good horn, but where's the challenge in that?

What to Look For

There are many things to look at when considering a trumpet, some obvious and some not so obvious. If you're buying a used horn and you know what to look for you can spot potential problems. If it looks like you know what you're doing and can tell the seller why a trumpet may not be perfect, often this will allow you to get the horn for a lower price.

If at all possible, take an experienced player with you to help you determine whether a trumpet is worth buying. Someone who plays can try out the horn and give it a more accurate assessment than a non-player or less-experienced player. Be sure to give whomever helps a thank you coffee or soda or snack for going along.

The Obvious: A trumpet should have at least one mouthpiece with it, but there is no guarantee that it will, so you should take a mouthpiece with you. Borrow one if necessary. Without a mouthpiece you won't be able to try the horn out, so put one in your pocket before you walk out the door. In fact, you should carry one everywhere anyway so you can practice your buzz.

Look for major dents or dings. Appearance aside, large dents will affect the airflow of the horn and its intonation. Some dings are easily removed by an instrument repairman and others are impossible to fix without taking the horn apart. Any dents to the valve casings are usually fatal to a horn, so if a trumpet has this problem, look elsewhere.

If a trumpet hasn't been used, the slides and valves may be frozen and won't move. This isn't necessarily a bad thing because most of these problems are easily fixed. If you aren't getting your trumpet from a music store, take along some valve oil so you can oil the valves if they need it. If you haven't oiled valves before, refer to the chapter in this book entitled, "Clean Up Your Axe" to learn how valves are oiled.

The Not So Obvious: Pull the tuning slide (if you can). If you can't pull the slide, ask the store owner to help you pull it. Once you get the slide out, look through the lead pipe. Digestion starts in your mouth with saliva, so saliva is pretty corrosive. The smoother the lead pipe the better. Older horns which have been played a lot may have pitting and scoring in the lead pipe, and sometimes the pipe may be worn all the way through. When this happens the lead pipe needs to be replaced.

If you aren't taking an experienced player with you, oil the valves and finger them randomly. You'll get a good idea if they'll stick by doing this. Try as many different combinations as you can. Fan each valve (push it up and down really fast) individually, then try them in combinations. If they stick, drop some more oil into them and try it again. If they still stick, there may be a problem. If you're serious about buying the horn, clean inside the valve casings and the valves and try it again (see the chapter on cleaning your horn to learn how to do this). If the valves still stick after this, don't buy the horn.

As a beginner, you may not want a horn that has a large diameter lead pipe (also called *bore*), because this will make it more difficult to play high and lessens endurance. The benefit to such an instrument is a fatter tone. If you have good air support and can get a good tone out of a larger bore instrument, you may want to get it anyway, because with practice you'll become a stronger player.

THE FINAL WORD

The best thing you could do when shopping for a trumpet is take along a trumpet player. The more experience that player has, the better, but anybody who knows more than you do would be an asset. This goes for not only the random trumpets at garage sales and pawn shops, but also the instruments in the music store, new or used. All trumpets are slightly different, even within a certain brand (Bach Stradivarius, for example), and a good player can tell the difference.

Keep looking if you don't find a horn immediately. Visit your local music store and sample a few horns to get an idea of what you might want and/or need.

Some folks have one horn and it's all they need. Others have vast collections. One of the most historic and interesting is the Utley collection. None of the instruments are for sale, but you can get an idea about what visiting garage sales in Europe will do to your closet space. Go to http://www.usd.edu/smm/Utley.html for a gander at some of these rare old trumpets.

MOUTHPIECE ANATOMY 101

If there is any one thing which will seriously affect your playing, it's having the correct mouthpiece. If you're a beginner you don't have to worry much about mouthpieces at first, but as you get better you may find that some mouthpieces work better than others. I've known players who had dozens of mouthpieces, though most players rely on a select few. Mouthpieces come in a bewildering array of shapes and styles, cup depths and shank lengths, density and diameter. It's enough to drive anyone but a brass player loopy.

Parts of the Mouthpiece

The Rim: This is where the mouthpiece meets your chops. A rounded rim gives a player more flexibility but tends to tire the lip more quickly. A flat rim allows for a sharper beginning to notes and adds brilliance to the sound but reduces flexibility. A wider rim provides better endurance, while a narrow rim provides more range. A sharp rim bite provides brilliance while a rounded rim bite is less brilliant but more comfortable.

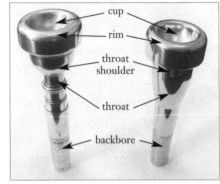

The Cup: The cup is measured by diameter and depth. The larger both are, the more resonant your tone will be. However, the larger a mouthpiece is, the more difficult it is to control. Also, a deep cup and wide diameter can make higher notes more difficult to play. The general idea is to use the largest cup you can without sacrificing ability or range.

The Throat Shoulder: This is where the air passes from the cup to the throat. The shoulder influences tone quality and resistance. Rounded shoulders are more resonant than sharper shoulders.

The Throat: This is the narrowest part of the mouthpiece. It's where the air moves from throat shoulder to backbore. A throat that is too small will make a trumpet play sharp up high, play flat down low, and feel stuffy. The bigger the throat the fuller the tone, but too big and it becomes difficult to play softly and endurance suffers.

The Backbore: The backbore is where the air passes from the throat to the lead pipe of the trumpet. Intonation and tone quality are affected by the backbore. A small backbore will give the sound a brilliance but at the cost of a flat, stuffy upper register. A large backbore can give a better tone, but too large and notes lack definition and you'll tire easily.

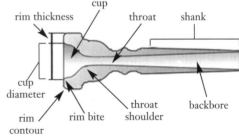

What to Look for in a Mouthpiece

The most general rule is to find the mouthpiece that is the most comfortable. It's that easy. The first critical question you should ask after finding a comfortable mouthpiece is, "Is it in tune?" If not, don't buy it. Be sure to take your tuner with you to the music store. If you don't have one, buy one at the music store. A tuner is a must.

Here's what instrument craftsman and mouthpiece designer Dave Monette has to say about choosing a mouthpiece (from *Monette Mouthpiece Manual and User's Guide*):

When selecting a new mouthpiece, the size that feels most comfortable and that allows you to play with the most easy, natural embouchure and in the most resonant, centered way is usually the best size for you!

If you are playing lead trumpet, use a lead mouthpiece! You would not run a marathon in wing tips, and you should probably not try and play the scream book in a big band on a B1-1 mouthpiece! (B1-1 is a very large mouthpiece.—JH)

If your sound shape is too narrow, you miss too many notes, and you have difficulties playing "down into the center" of the equipment, try a wider inside-rim diameter with a comfortable cup depth.

If your sound shape is too wide and you find yourself "swimming" in the equipment, try a narrower inside-rim diameter with a comfortable cup depth.

Flatter rims, or rims with more "bite" on the inside edge may provide more control and security in articulation, but too much "bite" or "grip" can inhibit flexibility. If you often "splatter" articulations, try a sharper rim. If you feel the rim constricts you, try a wider inside-rim diameter, a rounder rim contour, or both.

If a mouthpiece feels good, sounds good, provides better range and endurance, and plays more in tune, you have found your new mouthpiece—even if it is not what you are used to!

Mouthpiece Tips for the Very Confused

- Does the mouthpiece you are trying feel too wide or too narrow?
- Does the cup feel too shallow or too deep?
- Does the rim contour feel too round or too sharp?
- Do you need to take a break and come back to the process with a fresh perspective?

If after following these tips you still need help, find a teacher whose advice you trust, and purchase the mouthpiece he or she recommends. Then forget mouthpiece sizes and practice making music!

In the long run, players should always make a good mouthpiece selection based on what equipment helps them to sound better and make more music. If the process seems more complicated than that, you are making it more complicated than it needs to be.

7C, 3D, 2B? What Does It Mean?

Mouthpieces are usually stamped with a letter and a number, and each manufacturer has a slightly different definition of what these numbers and letters mean. The following chart may help clear up the confusion.

Generally, the number refers to the depth of the cup. A larger number *usually* means a shallower cup (see Laskey and Yamaha on the next page for exceptions). For instance, a Bach 7C mouthpiece (a good depth for a beginner) will have a much shallower cup than a Bach 1C.

Mouthpieces are not cheap, so most music stores will allow you to try out a mouthpiece before you buy. Bring your horn and tuner when shopping for a mouthpiece so you can try before you buy. Good luck!

In this chart, mouthpieces in the same row have roughly similar cup depth. Other characteristics like rim shape, backbore, etc., may be slightly different.

Bach	Giardi-nelli	Laskey	Marcin-kewicz	Monette	Schilke	Stork	Warb-urton	Yahama
1		84D		B1-1	19	1	1M	18C4
1B		84B	1	B1-5M			2D	17C4
1C		85C		B1-5	18			
1.25C		80MC		B2	17		2M	
1.5B		75B		B4	16			
1.5C		68C	1	B3	16		3M	16C4
2C	3M	70C		B4S	15	2C		15C4 or 16
2.5C			3					14A4a
3			4	B5				14A4a
3B		70B						13A4a
3C		65MC		B6	15		4M	
5C	5C or 6M	60C			13C4	3C		14C4
6							5MD	
6C					12		5MC	9C4
7					11A		6MD	8C4
7C	7C or 7M	50C	5-6	B7F	11		6MC	11 or 11C4
8C		50B	7-8			5C		
9C			9-10				6M	6A4a
10.5C	10M	40C	11-12	B8	9C4	7C	7MC	8C4
11C	12M		13-15		8A4		8MC	
17								
20C								

CHAPTER 2
WHAT THE BUZZ IS ALL ABOUT

It is possible to improve your trumpet sound almost immediately by working on the mouthpiece.
— Allen Vizzutti, trumpet master

What's Ahead:
- Forming the embouchure
- Buzzing
- Mouthpiece buzzing
- Buzzing exercises
- Mouthpiece information

Terms to Know:

embouchure (AHM-ba-sher): The position and use of lips, tongue, and teeth when playing a wind instrument.

buzz: The sound made when air is forced through a brass player's embouchure.

mouthpiece: On a brass or woodwind instrument, the part responsible for receiving the embouchure's vibrations. Placed on the lips for trumpet players.

aperture: The opening in your lips where the air escapes and the buzz happens. Aperture should not be too wide or too open.

chops: A cool word for "embouchure." Also refers to one's ability on an instrument.

ESCUCHA ME!

Before we start working on the lip buzz, please heed this important announcement: *Listening* is far and away the *very* best thing you can do for your trumpet playing ability and your musicianship skills. There is no substitute for it. Listening to music is food for your own music. If you don't listen to other players, your road to trumpet mastery will be long and lonely. That would be sad. Consider the words of the influential philosopher Friedrich Nietzsche: *Life without music would be a mistake*. Playing trumpet is not just about technique, it is about expression, saying something, *feeling* something and conveying it. To cultivate this awareness and ability, you must listen. In chapter 19, *Hear Here!*, you'll find a carefully selected list of great trumpet music by master musicians in many genres. Start listening now!

WHAT'S AN EMBOUCHURE?

All wind instrument players have an embouchure. Embouchure (AHM-ba-sher) is a French word meaning "the mouth of the river." In our case, the river is your airstream and the mouth of the river is *your* mouth. Embouchure in the trumpet world means the shape of your lips, tongue, and teeth when you play trumpet.

Learning how to form your embouchure is a crucial step in playing trumpet, and you want to get it exactly right or you may have problems later that will be hard to fix. When practicing your embouchure at first, do it with a mirror so you know you've got it right.

The cool word for embouchure is *chops*. After a long session of playing, you could say, "Man, my chops are sore!" In addition to referring to your mouth, chops can also mean your ability on an instrument. You could say, "Wow! Max Roach and Clifford Brown have monster chops!"

The Face Is the Place

The face is a unique place in the human body, especially the muscles that control it and allow you to grin, frown, scowl, raise an eyebrow, and of course, buzz your lips. Most muscles are connected to bones on each end, but not the facial muscles. These muscles are connected to your head bones on one end, but the other end is connected to soft tissue like the lips.

The lips aren't muscle. They're soft tissue. You can see this best in the diagram here. The lips don't do the work when playing trumpet. The surrounding muscles allow you to buzz your lips correctly and the most important ones are those at the corners of your mouth. Here's what they look like and their Latin names, which you are allowed to promptly forget, except buccinator: this word means *trumpeter* in Latin. It's an important muscle.

I'm showing you the chop muscles so that you understand it's the muscle doing the work and not

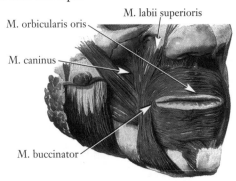

the lip. As with any kind of muscle building, it takes a *lot* of time, effort, and practice to teach the muscles to work efficiently. Think about how long it takes a bodybuilder to get their body to look like it does. If you consistently practice the exercises for building up your chops you'll get some dramatic results immediately. To get truly strong however, you'll build chop strength and efficiency over the course of a few years.

Dry vs. Wet Embouchure

The large majority of trumpet players wet their lips with their tongue before playing. This is called a "wet embouchure." Some players don't wet their lips before playing, and this is known as a "dry embouchure."

Why one or the other? With a wet embouchure, the lips will buzz more easily and it's easier to slide the mouthpiece to the best location. Those who use a dry embouchure say that it's easier to play higher and there isn't a lot of moisture interfering with the tone. Though most players use and recommend a wet embouchure, try both and see which one you prefer.

WHAT THE BUZZ IS ABOUT

All sound is vibration. With trumpet, the vibration is provided by the lips and the air column. The buzz is the sound your lips make which is then amplified by the trumpet into a gorgeous sound (with practice). Experience is worth a million words.

Take a deep breath. Lick your lips (or not, if you're using a dry embouchure), place them together as though you're saying "mmmm." Tighten the corners of your mouth and blow air through the middle of your lips. Use a LOT of air! From the middle of your lips you should get a funny buzzing sound caused by your lips vibrating together quickly. It's a lot like when you

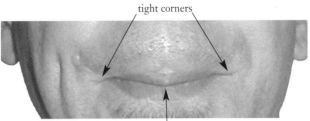

tight corners

the aperture: air escapes here, causing the "buzz"

pinch the neck of a full balloon and let the air out. Same principle. Your mouth should look something like this picture.

The *aperture* is the spot where the air escapes and the buzz happens. The aperture should be oval shaped and not too long across the lips or too open. Ideally, the aperture should be right in the middle of your chops, so strive for that. However, there are players who have an aperture somewhere other than right in the middle. If you can't get the aperture in the middle, check with a teacher to be sure your particular embouchure will work. It's tough to make changes once you have habits set in place.

Be careful to keep the soft, squishy, inner part of your lips from blowing outward like you're giving someone a raspberry. Strive for that "mmmm" type of lip formation. Some players find it helpful to keep the lips *slightly* rolled in.

When you practice the buzz, be sure to take deep breaths. For more information about breathing, see chapter 4, *Avoiding Bad Breath*. Your stomach will be quite firm when buzzing because you're using those muscles to push all the air in your lungs through the very small opening in your lips. It is a mistake however, to tighten your stomach muscles on purpose. Just blow and let your stomach muscles do what they do when you blow.

If you can't get a buzz at first, blow harder and try holding your lips more tightly together using the *corners* of your mouth. Look at the muscle diagram again and you'll see that the muscles just above and below the lip stretch parallel to the lip. Those muscles are meant to contract your lips together purse-string style, *not* to press them together. Use the corner muscles and the purse-string muscles against each other to create the necessary tension. Purse your lips and smile at the same time, or try to whistle and smile at the same time.

audio tracks 1

When you do get a buzz going, your lips might itch and tickle because you aren't used to vibrating your lips like this. The sensation goes away quickly, so keep at it. Check how the buzz sounds on track 1 of the CD. Here are the steps for making a buzz:

1. Look in the mirror and smile at yourself.
2. Take a deep breath.
3. Place your wet/dry lips together as though saying "mmmm." Keep the corners of your mouth tight, like you just had a big bite of lemon.
4. Force the air in your lungs through your lips. Use your stomach muscles to help push the air out.
5. Hold the sound of the buzz steady for as long as you can. Strive for a big, fat, steady sound.
6. Repeat for a few minutes. Don't forget to breathe.

You might find it difficult to get the buzz perfectly steady. Focus your attention on a steady air flow.

try this

Once you have a good buzz, do it for as long as you can in one breath. Strive for a clear, "fat" tone and a steady sound. Think "ten-pound bumblebee." Take another breath and do it again. Time yourself and keep a record of how long you can buzz before the muscles in your lips give out. It's a good idea to do this sitting down, and if you feel yourself getting dizzy and light-headed, stop for a minute or two until it goes away. *The buzz will strengthen your lips more than almost anything else you can do!*

The buzz is a very important aspect of playing trumpet and the better your buzz, the stronger your playing will be. I've heard *all* beginning players' tone improve with just a little buzzing.

Try to buzz high, low, and in between. Buzz continuously through your range from high to low. Try to buzz a simple song, like "Row, Row, Row Your Boat," or "Mary Had a Little Lamb." This will *not* be easy at first, but keep trying and it'll come. Try to increase your range both higher and lower. As simple songs get easier, try more difficult songs, like "Somewhere Over the Rainbow" from *The Wizard of Oz*. Don't neglect your buzz! You can do it anywhere.

Playing a wind instrument takes a *lot* of air and your nose is just too small to do the job right. When you take a breath while playing trumpet, DON'T breathe through your nose. Breathe from the corners of your mouth or drop your lower jaw and breathe through your mouth. Except in special circumstances, such as circular breathing, you'll *always* use your mouth to breathe.

BUZZ WITH THE MOUTHPIECE

Hold the mouthpiece with only your thumb and middle finger. Grasp it gently with these fingers placed near the end of the shank (the long tubular part). Look at the picture on the bottom of this page. Splay out your other fingers. Lick your lips (or not if you're using a dry embouchure), take a big breath, and place the mouthpiece directly over the buzz aperture. Ideally this should be close to the center of your lips, but it's not crucial. It's more important to center the mouthpiece over the aperture where your lips are buzzing. Blow just like you did when doing the previous buzz. The sound of the buzz through the mouthpiece is usually more clear and higher than the buzz without the mouthpiece.

Buzz with your mouthpiece. Repeat until airflow is smooth, your buzz tone is fat, and there are no gaps in the sound.

Don't press the mouthpiece into your lips very hard. Press just hard enough to make a seal so you aren't spraying air and spit out the corners of your mouth. As you start to play higher, you'll want to cram the mouthpiece into your face harder but *resist this*. The more relaxed you are, the better your sound will be. Playing without too much pressure is something most trumpet players struggle with at some point in their playing if they're serious about playing well. Get into the good habit of using the least amount of pressure you can get away with.

You'll find it's easier to produce a buzz with the mouthpiece. Buzzing with your mouthpiece can also be done almost anywhere, and a mouthpiece fits easily into a pocket. Do the same exercises with your mouthpiece as you do with the buzz alone: high, low, low to high and back to low, buzz simple songs, then harder ones.

At the end of this chapter are suggestions for buzzing exercises. Go through them once a day and you'll have a better trumpet tone and a stronger lip in a week or less. Trust me.

Holding the mouthpiece like this while buzzing will help you avoid using too much pressure.

Mouthpiece Placement

If you've been placing the mouthpiece in the center of the lips like the pictures show and not getting very good results, you might consider placing the mouthpiece elsewhere.

Remember that the ideal placement of the mouthpiece is where it sounds and feels the best. It's not crucial to place the mouthpiece in the center of the lips if this feels wrong to you. Some teachers insist on placing the mouthpiece in the center of the lips only, without regard to the shape of the student's face and teeth, and without regard to where the mouthpiece feels most comfortable to the student. Experiment with placement to hear where you get the best sound.

Cootie Williams, master of the plunger mute and trumpeter for Duke Ellington, played with an off-center embouchure and it certainly didn't hurt his career. If that doesn't convince you, you should know that Maynard Ferguson, master of the stratosphere, also plays slightly off center.

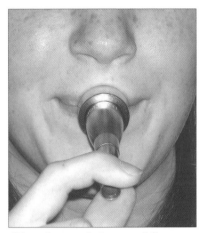

Place the mouthpiece carefully over your buzz. Placement should be where the 'piece is most comfortable and where you get the best tone. This may be in the center, as in this picture, or a little off center. Practice with a mirror!

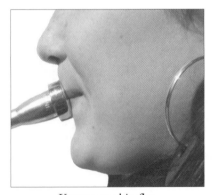

Keep your chin flat.
Use a mirror or a friend!

The Chin

The chin should be flat, not bunched up. While playing a long tone on the trumpet or with your buzz, reach up and feel your chin. If it *is* bunched up, pull it down so that it's flat. A good way to practice this is to form an embouchure without the mouthpiece, and be aware of your chin. Use your hand to check its flatness. When you can get a buzz with a flat chin, this will transfer to when you have the horn or mouthpiece on your face. Use a mirror.

BUZZING EXERCISES FOR STRONG CHOPS

Following is a short series of exercises to be done with the lip buzz alone *and* with the mouthpiece. The exercises take only six minutes (longer wouldn't hurt you) and are a great way to warm up and strengthen your lips before playing. At first, go through the whole series with just the lip buzz, then the whole thing with just the mouthpiece. Do one or the other every day. Both is better. After a week or so, mix and match. Make up your own.

If you're unfamiliar with reading notes, a note with an "x" as its head means the note has no specific pitch. If you'd like to learn more about reading music, check out *Basic Music Theory: How to Read, Write, and Understand Written Music.*

Each of these exercises has three or more variations of loudness: soft, medium, loud, and mixed. Try 'em all! At the Sol-Ut Web site (www.sol-ut.com) is a chart to keep track of exercises you're working on. Chart your progress with the buzz, and any other exercise. Post the chart in your case or practice room so you're reminded to do the exercises and so you can see your steady improvement.

Do exercises #1–5 with the buzz alone, then do them with the mouthpiece. If you do these daily, in a very short time you will possess much better tone and range. Do them with steady volume throughout, then add the crescendo (gradually louder) or decrescendo (gradually softer) when you're ready.

#1: The Long Buzz (1 minute)

BREATHE as needed, keep the tone as clear, fat and warm as you can. Listen very carefully. Do these in the low and middle register at both soft and medium loudness. Add a crescendo and decrescendo when you're ready.

#2: Start and Stop (30 seconds)

Don't stop the sound with your tongue—stop your air instead. Go slowly, BREATHE as needed, keep the tone as constant, clear, and fat as you can, and listen very carefully. Do these in the low and middle register at both soft and medium loudness. Add a crescendo and decrescendo when you're ready.

#3: High to Low (30 seconds)

Start at a high but comfortable pitch, and with a continuous sound, move slowly from high to as low as you can go. BREATHE as needed, keep the tone as constant, clear, and fat as you can, and listen very carefully. Do these at medium volume. You want a buzz that is constant and has no gaps in the sound. No gaps means your lips are warmed up.

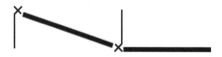

#4: High-Low-Middle (30 seconds)

Start at a high but comfortable pitch, keep the sound constant and go as low as you can with a good sound and hold the sound steady. Before you run out of air, go up to a mid-range pitch. BREATHE as needed, keep the tone as constant, clear, and fat as you can, and listen very carefully. Be aware that it is much more difficult to go from low to high than it is to go from high to low. Use fast air and chop strength, not mouthpiece pressure!

#5: The See-Saw (30 seconds)

Start at a high but comfortable pitch, keep the sound constant and go as low as you can and still maintain a pitch, go back up and try to get as high as your original note, then back down again. Repeat this until you run out of air. Don't use pressure to play high. BREATHE as needed, keep the tone as constant, clear, and fat as you can, and listen very carefully. Be aware that it is much more difficult to go from low to high than it is to go from high to low. Use fast air and chop strength, not mouthpiece pressure!

#6: Pitch-matching (Do with mouthpiece only)

Match these pitches (or choose your own) on piano or some other instrument. If you don't have access to a piano, use the CD. BREATHE as needed, keep the tone as constant, clear, and fat as you can, and listen very carefully. (More on music reading in chapter 6.)

Here are the trumpet notes as you'll find them on a keyboard. Use the keys right in the middle of the keyboard. If you already know the notes on the keyboard, you'll notice these names are different than what you know. To learn more about this, see *The Transposing Trumpeter* chapter in this book.

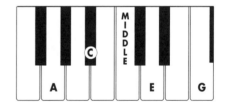

#7: Descending/Ascending Chromatic Scale (Do with mouthpiece only)

Buzz this scale down and then up. Hold each note for one full breath. Pause between notes. As you become more familiar with the sound of these notes, buzz the upcoming pitch *before* you play it on the piano.

Here are the trumpet notes as you'll find them on a keyboard. Use the keys right in the middle of the keyboard. If you already know the notes on the keyboard, you'll notice these names are different than what you know. For more information on transposing, see *The Transposing Trumpeter* chapter later in this book.

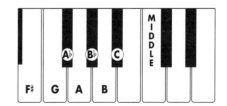

CHAPTER 3

LET'S GET IT STARTED

Don't be too timid and squeamish about your actions. All life is an experiment. The more experiments you make the better.

— Ralph Waldo Emerson (1803–1882)

What's Ahead:
- Putting your trumpet together
- How to hold it
- Posture
- Valves 101
- Simple exercises

Terms to Know:

valve casing: The metal which surrounds and supports the valves. The fingers of your left hand wrap around the valve casing.

trigger: Found on the third- and first-valve slides, these allow the fingers (ring finger and thumb, respectively) to move the slides in and out when necessary.

valves: The piston-shaped devices that divert air into the first-, second-, and third-valve slides, changing the pitch of the trumpet.

long tones: Any single note held out for one large, complete breath. Long tones should be clear and unwavering with a full tone.

mouthpiece puller: Pulls out the mouthpiece when it gets stuck.

FORGET THE DETAILS AND JUST GO FOR IT!

There are basically two types of learners: those who like as much information as they can get before they try something new and those who jump right in regardless of what they do or don't know. There are benefits to each approach.

If you're the type who loves to leap before looking, then by all means, go for it. Open your case carefully so you don't dump your horn on the ground (the lettering on the case should be upright and the latches usually open upwards). Pick up the horn and see if you can figure out how to hold it correctly. Put the mouthpiece in and give it a little twist when it's snug. Now blow! Put your buzz to work.

If you'd like to know before you blow, or if you had trouble with the guessing approach, read on.

THE DETAILS

If your slides and valves are in place, a trumpet is one of the easiest instruments to put together. Simply put the mouthpiece into the lead pipe snugly, give it a little twist to the left or right to lock it into place and you're ready to go! If your slides and/or valves *aren't* in place, skip ahead to the chapter on cleaning your horn to take care of that problem.

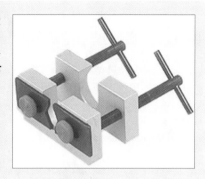

It's pretty easy to jam the mouthpiece in so that it won't come out at all, so be careful when you put the mouthpiece in. Don't tap or pound it in with your palm, and try not to drop your trumpet on the mouthpiece! If either of these unfortunate things does happen and you're unable to get the mouthpiece out (don't worry, this happens to most of us at least once), take it down to your local music store and their repair person will take it out for you. Most band directors also have a *mouthpiece puller* like the one by Bobcat shown here.

Hold It!

There are no hard and fast rules about how to hold the trumpet, but generally the trumpet is held around the *valve casing* by your left hand and the fingers of your right hand work the valves. Buddy Bolden, one of the great cornet players of New Orleans around 1900 (thought by many to be the first jazz musician), played left-handed. Most players stick to the standard because it's more comfortable. For various reasons, some people hold the trumpet other than the way I describe below. Do what's most comfortable and allows the horn to simply rest in your hand.

The Left Hand: To hold your trumpet correctly, wrap the fingers of your left hand around the valve casing. If your trumpet has a *trigger* on the third valve slide, put your ring finger in the trigger, wrap your index and middle fingers around the valve casing and rest your pinky wherever you want. Some third valve triggers are adjustable. If yours is one of these you can loosen the set screw and change the finger ring to a comfortable distance. Some trumpets have a trigger on the first valve slide too, and this is where your thumb goes.

Here's a picture of how I hold my trumpet. Some players put their pinky and ring finger under the third valve slide, wrapped around the valve casings. I played like this for many years, but switched my grip to allow my hand to be more relaxed. Your trumpet may be made differently than mine, and your hand may feel more comfortable in another position, so don't be afraid to experiment until you find what you like.

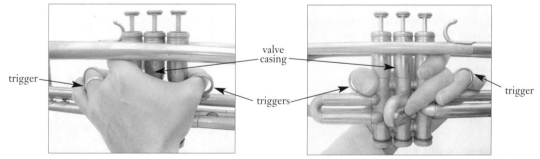

The left hand position: Strive for a relaxed hand. Don't grip the horn, let it rest in your hand.

The Right Hand: The first three fingers of the right hand go on the valves, slightly curved. Fingers are able to move much more quickly when they are slightly curved, like you're holding a tennis ball. Start this good habit right away. In addition, holding your fingers this way will help you avoid carpal tunnel syndrome, a painful and possibly long-lasting injury to the tendons which control the hand.

The pinky finger should rest on *top* of the finger ring, not hooked into it. This is very important. A common problem for trumpet players is using too much pressure against the mouth. With the pinky *inside* the finger ring, it's almost impossible not to yank the trumpet against your face, especially for high notes. This will cause problems! The finger ring is meant to be used to hold the trumpet with one hand while the other turns pages, works a plunger mute, picks your nose, or whatever. Don't use it as an octave key!

The correct way to hold your right hand. Take a close look at the right thumb and pinky.

The right hand thumb should rest in the little valley between the first and second valve. This is also to ensure your hand stays loose and relaxed, allowing the fingers to move quickly and easily. If you keep your thumb here you'll be less likely to grip the valves tightly, which not only slows down your fingers but also affects the quality of your sound. Again, this might be a little uncomfortable at first, but stick with it and soon it'll feel natural.

General Posture Info

Correct posture affects not only the body but the mind as well. You're more alert and able to concentrate when you sit or stand up straight. When playing a wind instrument, correct posture is even more crucial because it allows you to breathe correctly, and breathing is one of the most important aspects of playing trumpet. Whether sitting or standing, there are a few general ideas to keep in mind.

Bring the trumpet to your mouth and don't bring your mouth to the trumpet. If you bring your mouth to the trumpet, this will cause you to thrust your head forward slightly which will block your airflow. Check yourself in a mirror. Better yet, use two mirrors so you can see your profile, the angle of your trumpet, and the straightness of your head and neck.

Whether you're sitting or standing, imagine there is a string coming out the top of your head and it's being pulled up, almost lifting you off your chair or off the ground. This will keep your spine lengthened which will allow your lungs to expand fully and will also help to open your airway, improving airflow.

Relax your shoulders and keep your chest up and out. Think about your elbows. They should be relaxed and slightly out from your side. Don't clamp them to your side. Stay relaxed as much as possible.

Seated Posture

Arnold Jacobs, the phenomenal tuba player and master teacher, has good advice about the seated posture. He advises that you should sit in such a way that you can stand up immediately. This sounds simple but will probably take some adjustment before you're able to do it. Try it once right now. If you need to lean forward before you stand, you don't have it quite right. Keep your back off the chair and sit on the front half of the chair. Don't cross your ankles and keep your feet flat on the floor.

A study of master trumpeters' seated posture was done recently and when sitting, all the players' legs were at a 90-degree angle. This allowed the abdomen to expand freely and allowed the player

to take full advantage of the abdominal expansion necessary for a good breath. You should do this, too.

Another helpful item that will help your posture is a small wedge-shaped cushion. This type of cushion is often used in Iyengar yoga classes as a prop and you should be able to find one online or at a store that sells yoga gear. The cushion will help flatten your lower spine and possibly alleviate or forestall any back pain that may be a result of poor posture. Try it out and see what you think.

Standing Posture

When you stand up to play trumpet, a lot of posture problems are fixed automatically. It's easier to breathe deeply standing up and your sound will project through a room much better when you stand. When standing, place your feet hip width apart, toes pointed forward and knees slightly bent. Hips should be open. I can't stress enough how important all the things in the above sentence are. Do them! You will notice an immediate change in your sound, range, and endurance. All the previous advice also applies: chest up and out, elbows loose and relaxed, string pulling you up from the center of your head, and relax your shoulders. You may want to work with your teacher to be sure you've got the correct posture. Posture is that important.

Final Posture Tips

The exact angle to hold the trumpet is slightly different for everybody because of how your teeth are formed and how your specific embouchure is shaped. As a general rule, the trumpet should be angled slightly downward almost parallel to the ground

When starting something new, it takes time to form the correct habits. Check your posture as often as you can and fix it when you notice you're sagging or lopsided. Practice in front of a mirror. Have someone sneak a snapshot of you while playing. You might be surprised at your posture and will be more likely to correct it next time.

But again, posture isn't everything. If you look at Miles Davis, one of the best jazz trumpet players ever to live, you'll see that most times he pays little attention to correct posture, though he always looks relaxed. Zen master Shunryu Suzuki once said, "The secret of Zen is just two words: Not always so!" Try playing slouched over, play lying down on your back, standing on your head, under water, or any other way you can come up with. Simply stay relaxed, no matter what posture you're using. Be aware of how posture affects breathing. Always have fun!

Don't be afraid to try something different.

GO FOR IT!

By now, you're probably saying, "Enough with all the rules and suggestions! Just let me play the dern thing!" And that's just what you should do now and for the next week or two. Mess around with your horn and see what you remember from all your reading. It wouldn't hurt to review all this information midweek to see if you've got it perfectly or if you picked up a bad habit. Find and eradicate any bad habits as soon as you can because the longer you practice a bad habit, the tougher it will be to change. Following are some things to keep in mind or to try while messing around.

Stay Relaxed

Nothing will affect your sound more than the state of your body. A tense body will get tired more quickly and the sound produced by a tense body will also be tense and more difficult to control. Stay loose and relaxed. *Remember to be patient with yourself!*

Mental Checklist

Whenever you think of it, check these things:

- Finger position—right hand pinky and thumb especially. Curve those three fingers. Relax.
- Posture—edge of your chair if sitting, open hips if standing, feet shoulder width, string pulling you up, chest out, elbows relaxed and away from your side.
- Pressure on your lips (the less the better—use just enough pressure to get a good seal).
- Don't puff out your cheeks.
- Breathing (as deeply as you can).

Things to Try While Messing Around

- Take lots of breaks. *Rest as much as you play.*
- Play one note as long as you can in one breath. Time yourself and try to better your record each practice session.
- Make your sound go from loud to soft as smoothly as you can.
- Make your sound go from soft to loud as smoothly as you can.
- Play as low as you can.
- Play as loudly as you can with a good sound. Play as loudly as you can until the sound gets distorted.
- Play as softly as you can.
- Play as high as you can. Be careful here! It's easy to jam the trumpet on your face to play high, but resist the temptation! Play as high as you can without excessive pressure.
- Play from high to low with a continuous sound. This is called a glissando and is difficult for beginners, so use lots of air. Push the valves halfway down to make it easier, and for an interesting sound.
- Play from low to high with a continuous sound. This is even more difficult than going from high to low. Use half valves.
- If you get frustrated or bored, STOP. Give it a rest and pick the horn up later in the day or tomorrow.
- Congratulate yourself. You're playing trumpet!

Exercises to Get You on Your Way

Before we get into more complicated details about playing trumpet, there are several simple things you can begin to work on right away. Start perfecting these now and your sound and abilities will improve dramatically in just a few weeks.

Long Tones: You started to do these when you were messing around (see previous page). A long tone is any note you hold for a full breath. Make the sound as clean and steady as you can. Project your deepest, richest, clearest tone to the edges of the room. Really listen! By keeping your airflow steady you'll keep the pitch of the note steady.

Start and Stop: Start a note and hold it for a second or two. Stop the note with your air. Start the same note again and see if you can get it to sound immediately without any kacks or sputters or clams. Try it again with a different note. When you're good at doing this with just one note, choose a different note after stopping.

Trills: Play an open note (no valves down), then choose one valve to push up and down as fast as you can. Pay close attention to correct right hand position when doing this to get the most speed possible.

Listen: Have you listened to some good music today?

Finger Patterns: At sol-ut.com you can find finger patterns to practice.

CHAPTER 4
AVOIDING BAD BREATH

Virtually any aspect of trumpet playing will improve in direct correlation with improved breathing.

—Keith Johnson, *The Art of Trumpet Playing*

What's Ahead:
- Why learn to breathe?
- Taking a correct breath
- The breathing tube
- Breathing exercises
- Gadgets for better breathing

Terms to Know:

breath mark: An apostrophe-shaped (') symbol placed above the staff to indicate a breath is to be taken.

diaphragm: The muscle that controls the inhalation and exhalation of the lungs.

breathing tube: A tube of PVC, cardboard, or paper that help to open the throat for a good breath.

NB: No Breath. Don't breathe. Used as a reminder to avoid breaking a musical phrase with a breath.

WHY LEARN TO BREATHE? OR: I ALREADY KNOW HOW TO DO THIS...

The fact that the trumpet is a wind instrument is the first clue that wind, or breath, is an inseparable part of the instrument. Without your air the trumpet will make no sound at all. Your breath is as much a part of the instrument as the valves or mouthpiece is. If you start good breathing habits as soon as you begin playing, you'll make things much easier for yourself. The benefits of good breathing are better tone, better intonation, higher range, more endurance, louder louds, and softer softs. Sound good?

You might think breathing is such a natural thing that you don't really need to learn much more about it, but breathing for a wind instrument is special and needs to be done correctly if you want to be a good player. You can actually increase the amount of air you are able to take in, your *vital capacity*. Older players are especially encouraged to build their vital capacity with the exercises found in this chapter.

THE PHYSIOLOGY OF BREATHING

Breathing is usually done without thought. Your body knows what it needs to do and does it. However, unlike digestion and most other automatic bodily functions, you *can* take control of your breath. It's easy to hold your breath or take a deep breath or expel all the air out of your lungs. Controlling the breath is important because taking a breath for trumpet playing is different from normal breathing. At first you'll need to be very conscious of what you're doing. It can be valuable to know exactly what is happening in your body when you breathe.

There is a rhythm generator in your brain which fires about 12 times a minute, on average, for your entire life. This happens for reasons not completely understood. This rhythm helps your brain know when it's time to breathe. When it *is* time to breathe your brain sends an electrical impulse down your phrenic nerve to your diaphragm, the muscle which controls inhalation and exhalation.

The diaphragm is the main muscle of breathing. It stretches across the chest from side to side and front to back. When you inhale, the diaphragm contracts downward. This creates a vacuum in the lungs which draws air down into them. When the air enters the lungs, something has to be displaced to make room for it. That something is the rest of your innards: stomach, liver, intestines, etc. So when you take a deep breath, your stomach should push out. Here's a diagram to help with the visualization. Take a breath or three and try to feel what is going on inside.

One of the reasons this diagram is helpful, is that it shows what happens to your guts when you inhale. Stress and not wanting to look "fat" cause us to breathe shallowly, up high in our chests. As you can see, when you take a full, deep breath, your abdomen *has* to expand outward to make way for all the air you're taking in. If you want to play trumpet well, you have to learn how to take a good breath. This will take some time and concentration, but keep at it! Work with your teacher.

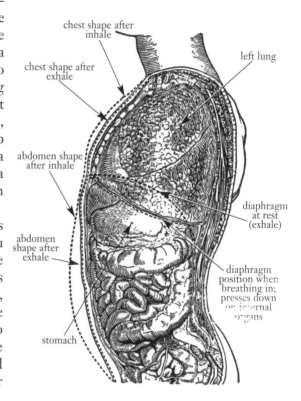

chest shape after inhale

chest shape after exhale

left lung

abdomen shape after inhale

abdomen shape after exhale

diaphragm at rest (exhale)

diaphragm position when breathing in; presses down on internal organs

stomach

THE CORRECT BREATH

A large breath can be thought of as a three-step process, with the first step being the most difficult to learn. It's not really *that* difficult. It's more about awareness than anything else; awareness of what your body is doing, awareness of what you want to accomplish, and awareness of whether you've accomplished it.

An important aspect of the correct breath is posture. The less flesh that is in the way of the incoming air the better. If you're slouched over, this will cramp your lungs and they won't be able to expand to their full capacity. If your head is tilted left or right, up or down, your throat will be constricted and you won't be able to get the maximum amount of air through. Inhalation should be quiet. If you hear noise on your inhale, your throat is in the way. Sit or stand tall, jaw level with the floor, and chin slightly tucked in. You can also try thrusting your jaw forward a little to help open the throat.

The Proper Breath, Step 1

When we are babies we breathe like a trumpet player should. As we get older, the tensions of living in the world cause our breathing to become shallower, up high in our chests. If you've watched a baby breathe, you've probably seen their little stomach push out with the inhale and go back in on the exhale. That's how it's supposed to be, and that's the first step of the three-part full breath. It's the most important part, too, so practice until it's automatic. I've been playing trumpet for more than 25 years, and I still try to remain conscious of this part of the deep breath.

The following preliminary exercises can help you feel what should happen during the first stage of a proper breath:

1. Lie on your back and relax; rest your hand on your stomach and take a deep breath. Your hand should rise up as your lungs fill and the air displaces the rest of your innards. If this doesn't happen, you're breathing shallowly up in your chest and your shoulders are probably moving. Keep practicing.

2. Sit in a chair and lean over until your chest is resting on your lap. Take a deep breath. Stay in this position through several breaths and feel where your body is expanding. Place your hand on your lower back and take another breath. You should feel your body expanding even back there. You should feel the pressure around your midsection, from your belly to your back.

3. Now sit or stand and try to breathe in the same way. Can you do it? Do you feel your body expanding in the same places? If not, keep practicing until you can. This is the most important part of the breathing process. Practice deep breathing wherever you are, whenever you think of it, until it becomes habit. This is one of the most important things to learn as a wind player!

Proper Breath, Step 2

It's important to wait on Step 2 until you've got Step 1 down *very* well. This is because Step 1 will give you much more air than any of the other steps. Also, Step 2 is where we usually breathe, up higher in our chest, and it's easy to do only this part and neglect Step 1. Don't neglect Step 1!

After your abdomen pushes out and your lower lungs are filled as much as they can be, lift your chest up and out and you'll find you can continue to fill up with more air. Your upper chest will expand in this stage, but not nearly as much as your abdomen did in Step 1.

Proper Breath, Step 3

There is some debate as to whether this part of the process is necessary. Some use it, some don't. Bobby Shew teaches it, so it certainly can work. Decide for yourself. The reason this step is debated is because it involves the shoulders rising, which is usually the sign of a shallow breath.

In the third step you're filling up the very top of your lungs and this causes the shoulders to rise slightly. If done correctly, the shoulders will rise all by themselves because of the continued expansion of the lungs. Some people help a little by raising the shoulders, then lowering them to add compression when they play, especially for loud or high playing.

All Together Now, 1-2-3

It takes a whole lot more time to explain this type of breath than it does to perform it. At times this breath has to be very fast, and even when you have the time it should take less than two seconds to fully tank up on air.

In order to do this breath quickly, your throat must be open. Check your posture, maybe push your jaw forward a little, and go through the three stages slowly at first, then more quickly until it's automatic and fast. There is a tool called a *breathing tube* which will help get your throat open and help to speed up the process. Learn about it on the next page.

Spend time at the beginning of each practice session to focus on breathing correctly. This means doing the exercises above, using the breathing tube which is explained next, and doing the following breathing exercises.

The Breathing Tube

This isn't a snorkel. It's a piece of 1-inch PVC tubing (or any type of tube, like the cardboard in a roll of toilet paper or a rolled-up file card) which will help teach you how to take a good breath. I have my students wear one around their neck and use it for a few years or until the breath is good and big and automatic. I still use mine during warm-ups to remind myself.

Place the tube in your mouth over your tongue and put it at least an inch or more into your mouth. This may be uncomfortable at first, but as long as you don't gag, you'll be okay. If you *do* gag, I apologize. Don't put the tube in quite so far. Okay, your tube's in? Now take a *slow* three-step breath. Exhale. Now do a *quick* three-step breath.

Did you feel how quickly you got a lungful of air? The air should fall right into your lungs quietly, with very little effort and nearly instantly. This is what taking a good breath feels like. Practice slowly, going through all three stages. Speed up until you can do this quickly. As you practice, you might want to sit down because taking in this much air will probably make you feel light-headed. If this happens, wait until the feeling passes before you continue.

SOME BREATHING EXERCISES

1. Sit-ups. Yes, something as simple as sit-ups will help improve your breathing. Playing trumpet not only involves breathing, but also blowing and sometimes blowing very hard. Strong stomach muscles are essential to blowing on trumpet when playing loudly. Plus, doing sit-ups is good for your lower back. In fact, exercise in general is great for your trumpet playing and your life. Do some today!

2. Take a piece of typing paper and draw a bull's-eye in the center of it. Hold the paper out right in front of your face and blow towards the center of the bull's-eye as though you were blowing soap bubbles through a wand. When the paper moves outward, hold it steadily with your air so it doesn't flutter around. Do this several times and be sure to sit or take a break, or both, if you begin to get dizzy or light-headed. Gradually move the paper further out with each new breath until the paper is at arm length. It will be more difficult to keep the paper pushed back and steady the further away it is, but keep the air flowing and you'll have good success. Tape the paper to a stand so you can back up further. Continue backing up to about 10–15 feet or until the paper doesn't move. The distance you'll be able to move the paper will increase the more you practice this exercise.

3. This is a more difficult version of #2: Sit in front of a candle in a windless room. Take a correct deep breath and blow. Focus your airstream on the candle and try to bend the flame without blowing it out. As with the paper, keep the flame bent back to the same spot and don't let it waver. This will take some practice to perfect. Back up and do it again. See how far away you can be and still affect the flame (10–15 feet is good). Keep at it. The benefits are worth it even if you can't feel them yet.

4. Set up a metronome to beat at MM=60, or keep track of the seconds on a watch. Breathe in fully and deeply for two beats (two seconds), then focus your airstream like you did with the bulls-eye exercise and blow for six seconds. Get rid of *all* your air by the time the sixth beat ends, take another two-beat breath and do it again. After two repetitions, increase the "blow" count to seven and do that twice also. Increase the count to eight, then nine, then ten. Do each twice. Learn to conserve your air and use as much of it as you can in the time given. If you start to feel light-headed, stop until the feeling passes.

5. Breathe in for two counts, focus your airstream, and get rid of all your air in five counts as before. Two beats of deep inhale, and exhale all of your air in four beats, then inhale two and blow three, then inhale two and blow two, and finally inhale one and blow for one. Repeat each twice. Keep your airstream focused, like you're blowing soap bubbles. It will be much more difficult to get rid of all that air in one beat. Your stomach muscles should get a nice little workout with this exercise. This one will also probably make you light-headed, so be careful.

6. Hold a small piece of paper against the wall, stand back about six inches, take a good three-step breath and blow. Hold the paper against the wall with your airstream. Take a breath and move back an inch or two (hold the paper with your hand as you breathe in). Back up with each new breath. How far back can you stand and still hold the paper against the wall?

7. So far you've had no resistance to your exhale. Playing trumpet involves resistance to the exhale. Take a deep breath and exhale (three times). Then after the inhale, blow through the trumpet without the mouthpiece (three times). Then blow three times through the mouthpiece alone (no embouchure). Then put the mouthpiece in the horn and blow three more times (still no embouchure). Finally form an embouchure (but don't make a buzz!) and blow three more times after a good three-step breath. You should feel the resistance increase with each step in this exercise.

WHEN TO BREATHE

When to take a breath is an important skill to learn because it can't happen just anywhere. Because a breath takes some time even at its fastest, and because your horn won't make any sound as you inhale, it's important to put the breath where it won't interfere with the melodic (or harmonic) phrase. If you took a breath in the middle of a phrase, that would be like saying a sentence with a bunch of pauses in it and that would be distracting.

Some music, especially for beginners, is marked with what are called *breath marks* which look a lot like commas (') and are written near the top of the staff. Often when you write them in your music, it's to remind yourself to take a large breath so you can make it through a phrase. The larger the breath you need, the larger the breath mark is drawn. And if you don't pay attention to it, you can make it bigger, circle it, highlight it, or whatever else it takes.

On the other hand, there are also times when you need to break the habit of breathing in the wrong place which will chop up the musical phrase. In this case, write a large **NB** where you usually take the forbidden breath. This stands for—you guessed it—**No Breath**.

WHEN YOU HAVE TOO MUCH AIR

Oboe players have a very difficult job. They have to take big breaths but because they're pushing their air through a tiny little reed, they almost always have extra air in their lungs. They not only have to breathe in, but they also have to breathe *out* to get rid of the old stale air. You'll also have to do this occasionally, but lucky for you not as often as oboe players.

It's important to have a good volume of air in your lungs to get the compression you need to play. But once that air is used up by your body, you have to get rid of it and replenish it with fresh air. The longer you play, the more you'll learn to use you air and identify such places. Use your judgment.

USING GADGETRY TO INCREASE BREATH AWARENESS

It's fun to mess around with odd-looking contraptions, especially if they help you breathe better. The breathing tube was a very simple gadget compared to what comes next. These gadgets will help you become more aware of your breath. They're great tools to get you thinking about your lung capacity, your state of relaxation, lengths of inhales and exhales, and other important aspects of a good breath.

Apply what you learn with these tools to playing on the horn. A good teacher can and should help you with this, and a good teacher will probably have some of these devices. Even with the greatest teacher in the universe, it's still ultimately up to you. A good breath is a habit you must work to develop and continue to monitor.

Watch the bouncing ball. Most of these devices use a ping-pong-like ball which rides on the column of air you provide, whether you're inhaling or exhaling. For your own version of this, try putting a ping-pong ball on your mouthpiece cup. Carefully blow through the shank of the mouthpiece and you'll notice the ball will "stick" there in any position, as long as you're exhaling. All devices in this chapter can be purchased from WindSong Press at www.wind-songpress.com/products.htm. On to the gadgetry!

The Voldyne

I chose this one first because it has a cool name, like something out of an old Flash Gordon movie. The Voldyne allows you to check the strength and volume of your inhalations. It has two chambers which measure air volume and pressure. There is a gauge which tells you how many milliliters of air you can take in and a marker which marks the high point of your lung capacity.

Before you inhale, empty your lungs completely so you'll get a more accurate measure of your lung capacity. When you inhale, do it as quickly as you can. This will measure the strength (pressure) of your inhale. A Voldyne will set you back about $17.

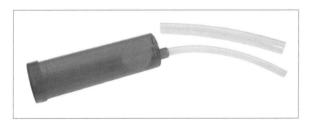

The Breath Builder

The breath builder was invented by bassoonist Harold Hansen and is a tube with a ping-pong ball in it and a smaller, straw-like tube coming from the top. The tube has three holes in the top so you can vary the resistance.

You inhale or exhale into the tube and the ball goes up to the top of the tube and stays there as long as you're inhaling or exhaling at the minimum amount of pressure (14 ounces). The device helps to maximize inhalation and exhalation and is also a great way to practice keeping your airflow steady and smooth. They cost around $18.

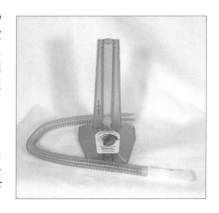

The Inspiron

Another Flash Gordon name. This device is also known as the incentive spirometer. A friend of mine had a collapsed lung and when I went to visit him in the hospital, he had one of these devices next to his bed to help him recuperate. The Inspiron allows you to visualize how much air you can inhale and, when you turn it over, how much air you can exhale. There is also a gauge to help measure resistance.

The Inspiron also has a ping-pong ball which measures your lung performance. Set the resistance to maximum, inhale, and move the ball to the top of the column. Just before the exhale, turn the device over. A mouthpiece can also be attached to the tube for further study. Cost is about $16.

The Air Bag

This is a simple device which allows you to see how much air you're able to hold in your lungs. The bags come in 5 and 6 liter varieties and will give you a rough idea of your vital capacity. A benefit to using the air bag for several breaths in row is that you'll avoid hyperventilation by re-breathing air that has less oxygen in it. An air bag costs about $25.

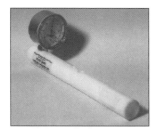

Variable Resistance Compound Gauge

This is a device invented by Arnold Jacobs and is used to measure the inhalation/exhalation cycle. Its use will also train you to increase both the inhalation and exhalation. The device will help you increase your actual vital capacity. After practicing with the VRCG, go back to the Voldyne and you should notice improved capacity. Of all these devices, this one is the most expensive, around $100.

AN ENCOURAGING WORD

Stick with this breathing thing. Get feedback from your teachers, either your teacher at school or your private teacher. Get feedback from other players, too. Often other people who are wrestling with the same things you are will give you insight into what you're trying to accomplish. Talk with other interested musicians about these things. Your education is out there, and you don't necessarily have to have a teacher to get it. Just pay attention and ask questions and experiment with yourself. Thich Nhat Han said, "This life is the instrument with which we experiment with Truth." Get out there and experiment!

CHAPTER 5

THE PRACTICE OF PRACTICE

I never practice; I always play.

—Wanda Landowska, 1952

What's Ahead:

- Where to practice
- When to practice
- How to practice
- What to practice
- Why practice?
- Warm-up exercises

Terms to Know:

'shed: As in "woodshed." A slang term hip musicians use to mean practice. As in going out to the woodshed and really working on your music.

etude: (AY-tude): A piece of music studied to improve technique.

metronome: A mechanical device used to keep perfect time.

tuner: A mechanical device used to monitor correct pitch.

pedal tone: A note below the normal range of the trumpet. Excellent for warming up the chops.

NB: No Breath. Don't breathe. Used as a reminder to avoid breaking a musical phrase with a breath.

PRACTICE OR PLAY?

If playing an instrument well happened by wanting it badly enough, there would be many more great musicians in the world than there are. That's not how it works, is it? To learn an instrument you've got to practice.

I don't really like the p-word. When I think of the word "practice," what usually comes to mind is a boring task, one which I'm forced to do repeatedly. I prefer a friendlier p-word. Play. Another cool word for practice is *'shed*, as in going out to the woodshed to play.

In order to do something well, you have to spend a lot of time doing it. This may seem obvious, but you'd be surprised by how many students—especially the younger ones—don't quite understand this. Whether it's sports or art or business or any old thing you care to name, to become something more than a beginner takes focused effort and some time. According to Dizzy Gillespie, it takes ten years of practicing your butt off to achieve mastery (we can assume he meant mastery of bebop). His statement has been backed up by scientific research which shows that to reach a very high state of mastery, a task should be repeated about a *million* times, which takes about ten years. Better get busy if artistic mastery is your goal!

Be aware, however, that repetition alone is not enough. The best music expresses something ineffable. Some call it feeling, emotion, or aesthetic experience, and some choose not to define deeper musical experiences so specifically. Simple repetition simply won't allow you to make music, though it may give you great technique on the instrument. Think about the best music you know and how it makes you feel. *That's* what you're after. There is a Zen saying that sums it up perfectly: Do not follow in the footsteps of the wise. Seek what they sought.

A Note on Private Teachers

No book can teach you everything or teach it as well as a good private teacher can. The fastest way to learn anything is one-on-one, just you and the teacher in a room. Half an hour each week is pretty standard for beginners, but an hour is better. A good trumpet teacher can save you years of time and show you tricks that make playing much easier and more rewarding. A good teacher knows what songs you can handle, knows which ones are fun, and will show you things you aren't doing quite right as well as how to do them better. A good teacher also provides positive feedback and encouragement to you, the student. This is perhaps the most valuable asset of a teacher. If you are not receiving a majority of these things in your lessons, consider another teacher.

A *good* teacher is invaluable. Find one. Study with him or her until you've soaked up all you can (usually 2–4 years), then find another and do it all over again. You'll learn the most this way, the fastest this way, and you'll never regret the money you spend. It's well worth it.

Good teachers aren't cheap though, and if you can't afford one you have several options. One good alternative, especially if you're a beginner, is to find someone who plays your instrument and is further along than you are (high school and college students work well). Another way is to find musicians that will let you hang out with them while they play. You can pick up a lot of free tips this way, often just by listening and watching.

COME ON BABY, LIGHT MY FIRE!

The single most valuable thing you have to stoke your musical fire is your desire to play music. Foster it. Imagine yourself playing somewhere. Anywhere. You could be on stage in front of 10,000 screaming fans, you could be at Carnegie Hall, you could be at the local coffee shop, you could be playing a song for a loved one or even in a room alone playing for yourself. There are many excellent players in the world who play only for personal enjoyment. Use your imagination to see yourself performing, keep with it, and you'll get to experience it!

Desire will keep you motivated through exercises and repetitions and slumps in mood. The only problem with desire is that it's not like a metronome. You can't bop down to the local music store and pick some up, so you've got to foster it, be aware of it, help it grow. You can't buy it, but there are ways to increase it. Live music is best, but great recordings are essential for focused study. Detailed discographies appear in chapter 19, *Hear Here!*

> *Take a music bath once or twice a week for a few seasons, and you will find that it is to the soul what the water bath is to the body.*
>
> —Oliver Wendell Holmes, Jr.

HOW TO GET BETTER

This is what practice is all about and there are ways to maximize the speed at which you improve. Here are just a few suggestions. If you're a beginner, it's essential to take things slowly. As a beginner you're trying to get the hang of a very complex task that involves many different and challenging skills, and it takes time. Stick with it. You'll get it. I have *never* run into someone who has said, "Gee, I'm sure glad I quit playing my trumpet." It's always the opposite. Tack up encouraging notes to yourself. On my music stand I have a fortune cookie message which says, "Be persistent and you will win."

As a beginner, your playing sessions might be ten to fifteen minutes, three or four times a week. The less you play, the longer it will take to get better. Remember this. It seems to be common sense, but I see it all the time with new students—playing is difficult and unfamiliar at first so they don't play much or not at all and it *remains* difficult and unfamiliar and frustrating. **The less you play, the longer it will take to get better.** There is no getting around this. Once a week will simply not cut it. Of course, once a week is better than nothing, but it's too easy to forget over a week's time and when you get back to your instrument, very little will have changed. This will be very frustrating. Avoid frustration by playing more often. Am I repeating myself? Yes, I am. Pick that thing up and put some sound into it!

Play as long as you can, but don't push it too hard. Remember that the best indication of when it's time to stop is your frustration/boredom level, or the soreness of your chops. You have your whole life to work on this. Don't be lazy, but don't overdo it either.

If you're taking private lessons, the very best time to practice is right after a lesson while that information is still fresh in your head. Record your lesson or take notes if you can't play immediately afterwards.

Don't Beat Yourself Up

Remember that it usually takes a long time to sound *really* good, and the progress is incredibly gradual. Anyone who plays an instrument has been a beginner at one point, and let's be honest—beginners make some really funny noises: squeaks, blats, bellows, and bleats. We've all done it. It's part of the process of becoming better. Have the patience to wait out your frustrations and the funny sounds you might make. Things will get better, I promise they will, but only if you stick with it. But as a beginner it *is* possible to get a beautiful tone out of a trumpet. Work on that first.

TeeVee

My first piece of advice is to throw the time bandit out. No? You're unwilling to do that? Okay then, use it to your advantage. During one hour of prime time television there are over twenty minutes of advertisements. That's twenty minutes you could use to play. And besides, you don't need to buy all that stuff people are trying to sell you. Save your money and buy a nicer trumpet instead, or some great recordings. Press the mute button and play! (This technique also works best for single people, or those with a good practice mute…)

When in Doubt, Leave It Out

I leave most of my instruments out and ready to play. I have to be careful when I pick one up because once I do, often it's tough to put it down again. By leaving your instrument out you can pick it up at a random moment and toss off an exercise or a song. If you do this with trumpet, be sure that you have already performed a warm-up at some earlier time. Five minutes later you're back to what you were doing before. You can find a trumpet stand at your local music store.

WHERE TO DO IT

When I was a kid learning to play trumpet, my parents ended up sending me to the garage to play. It might sound cruel, but it was an excellent thing. They didn't have to hear my squawks, blats, and repetitious patterns and *I* didn't have to feel self-conscious about making so much noise or repeating a scale for the umpteenth time. The garage also gave me the privacy to really explore the sounds I could pull out of the instrument.

When you start to play an instrument as a beginner, your self-image as a musician is very fragile. You'll feel self-conscious, maybe a little silly, and you'll be very aware of how bad you sound.

Yes, it's true. You *will* sound bad at first. That's part of it. For some it can feel embarrassing, and for others simply uncomfortable. Only a rare few don't care. If you're one of these, consider yourself lucky. If you do feel uncomfortable playing with others around, the solution is to play when you have lots of privacy, either when nobody else is home or in a separate building. Even a closed door is better than nothing.

Repetition: The Mother of Success and the Father of Irritation

Charles Reynolds, a master teacher and man of great enthusiasm coined the first part of the above phrase, and I added the second. When you're learning to play a song, you must play it over, and over, and over, and over, often hundreds if not thousands of times. And not the whole song at once, but measure by measure until you've got the whole thing. Then you get to play the whole thing over and over and over.

It's a lot like jet skis—plenty of fun for the one doing it but not fun at all for anyone who has to listen to it. Even if you've got the chops of Wallace Roney or Charlie Schlueter, the same phrase or scale or exercise played over and over and over again will drive even the most patient person bug-nuts.

Get a private place to play if you can. Those you live with will love you for it and will enjoy your music more when you're ready to perform it for them.

HOW TO DO IT

There are as many ways to play as there are people who play, but all of them share some similar characteristics. There are certain tools which can make your progress on trumpet much faster. Some of these tools are crucial, some are less so, but all of them will put you further down the road toward trumpet and musical mastery if you use them correctly.

All you really need is your instrument and desire. The rest will come. However, here are some things which will make your experience much more pleasant and more successful in a shorter time. In order of importance they are:

instrument: Get the best instrument you can afford and treat it well. Learn how to care for your trumpet in chapter 14, *Clean Up Your Axe.*

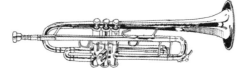

metronome: Apart from your instrument, this is the most useful tool you can own as a musician. Get one early and use it often. I'll discuss its use later in this chapter.

written music: This is both method books and sheet music. Not every playing session will require music. Many things can be done without it.

music stand: There are many different types, from inexpensive 15-dollar wire stands which fit in an instrument case to beautiful and expensive hardwood stands which aren't so portable.

pencil: This will be used to mark up your music with notes to yourself and also to record your sessions if you choose to do so. Keep several in your case so you'll have one when needed.

practice journal: A spiral notebook in which to keep a record of what you play, how long you play, and how you feel about your playing. This is a valuable tool to look back on. Not a requirement, but a good idea.

tape/CD player: A very useful tool. Not only to provide good music to listen to, but also something you can play along with. Trying to figure out a favorite song is good training for your hand-ear coordination. There are many recordings which leave out the trumpet part so you can play it.

tuner: A tuner can tell you exactly what pitch you play, and whether it's in tune or not. You're now in the world of sound and a small change of pitch is audible to most listeners. Certain notes on the trumpet are notoriously out of tune. With a tuner you'll know how much to correct them. For more information, see "Basic Trumpet Tuning" on page 76.

tape recorder: Not essential, but very helpful. Hearing yourself recorded is much different than hearing yourself while playing, and you'll be surprised how many mistakes you hear that you weren't aware of while you recorded. The tape recorder tells no lies.

instrument stand: Not essential, but useful. If you leave your trumpet out you'll pick it up and play more often. My trumpet, guitars, and flutes are always out on their stands.

THE IDEAL PRACTICE SESSION

A great practice session is divided into three sections:
1. The warm-up: warming up the horn and yourself physically and mentally.
2. Technical exercises: scale studies, lip slurs, tonguing, and a million other things to work on.
3. Musical material: etudes, orchestral excerpts, songs, or whatever it is you'll be performing. This is where you get to really play and this should be the most enjoyable part of your session.

Rest as much as you play! Trumpet is a physically demanding instrument. The muscles used for trumpet are small muscles that tire easily. Piano players can play for many hours in a day because they're using large muscles which don't tire like your face does. Resting while practicing trumpet is crucial!

As a general rule, you should rest as much as you play. Resting means not having the horn on your face. This doesn't mean that you should just stare at the wall while you rest. Use the down time to practice fingerings, tap out a difficult rhythm, sing some of your parts, oil your valves, or whatever is most helpful. During your play time, try to be actively learning *something* when the horn isn't on your face.

The Best Time: Directly after a lesson is the very best time to practice. When all that new information is fresh in your head, take the time to go over it again on your own. If there is something you don't understand, write down any questions or problems you may have so your teacher can explain them in your next lesson.

Pre Warm-up

Anne Morrow Lindbergh said, "A note of music gains significance from the silence on either side," and in that spirit, take a few seconds or a minute to sit quietly and think about your progress on trumpet, your goals, and how you will chip away at them during this practice session. This is an important and helpful way to start your session because it gets you mentally prepared and focused.

Then make sure your instrument works properly and you have all you need for the coming session (metronome, valve oil, metronome, music, metronome, mutes, pencil, etc.—don't forget your metronome).

A good way to get blood flowing to your lips and to get your air moving is to do the loose lip flap. This sounds a little funny, kind of like a horse whinny or an outboard boat motor, but is great for loosening up your mouth and lips. Keep your lips loosely closed and blow lots of air through them. This is not like the buzz because the lips are MUCH looser. Do this for 15 to 20 seconds.

Take a proper three-step breath and blow warm air through your horn to warm it up. See "Some Breathing Exercises" on page 27. This will help you think of the proper way to breathe while you warm up the horn. The pitch of a cold horn is lower than the pitch from a warm horn, so if being in tune is important to you (it should be), the horn must be warm before it can be in tune.

The Warm-up

A warm-up is essential for trumpet players. Not only does a good warm-up get the blood flowing to your chops, a warm-up also gets your mind focused and helps with your concentration as you go through your session. This is general information. Specific music for warm-ups can be found at the end of this chapter. See "The Practice Session Details" on page 38.

Start buzzing with your lips alone. If you're a beginner, just buzz a steady, comfortable note. As your muscles get stronger, you can vary the pitch. Go from a steady mid-range note to a low note. Go from high to low and low back to high. Experiment.

Buzzing on the mouthpiece is also a great way to warm up. Just like buzzing without the mouthpiece, experiment to find your own variations. Keep the range low and the volume medium to loud with little to no pressure on the lips from the mouthpiece. Buzz for a couple minutes until you have no gaps or stops in the sound. Check chapter 2 if you need reminders about the buzz.

FREQUENTLY USED PRACTICE TOOLS

The Metronome (or: The Torture Device)

A metronome is a mechanical foot tap which keeps perfect time. Each metronome has a series of gradations on it, usually from around 40–200 *beats per minute* (bpm). The higher the number, the faster the clicks. You set the metronome on the tempo you need and away you go.

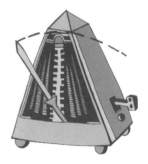

Metronomes come in many different shapes and sizes. Because trumpet can be such a loud instrument, you want the battery-operated version with an earplug that will send the clicks right to your ear. This is also a good option if you live with others: the repetitive clicks of a metronome can send others to the loony bin.

Nobody likes being wrong. That's one of the reasons metronomes are so neglected. They keep perfect time and we humans do not. We learn the most when we're wrong, as long as we're paying attention. So really, being wrong can turn into a good thing. Of course *staying* wrong is *not* a good thing. Use a metronome to help fix mistakes in rhythm.

How to Use the Metronome

When you're learning a song, use the metronome on only a short section at one time—several measures at the most, two notes at the least. It's important to *start slowly*. Whatever you learn is what you will play, so *if you set the metronome at a speed which is too difficult, you will learn mistakes.*

1. Set the metronome to a tempo that is slow enough so your playing feels comfortable and easy. Play the short section through a few times at this tempo. If you're making mistakes, the tempo is too fast. Slow it down some more until you find an easy tempo. Play five to ten times correctly before going on.

2. Click up to the next fastest tempo. One click only. The clicks may not *sound* any faster, but when you play the passage you'll notice the difference. Play at this tempo until it's easy. Play five to ten times perfectly.

3. Click up to the next fastest tempo. One click only. Play the section several times at the new tempo. It may take more repetitions to get the passage perfect. Keep at it. If it's too hard at the new tempo, go back one click until it's perfect again. Play five to ten times perfectly.

4. Continue with this process until the correct tempo of the song is reached. This may take several days, weeks, or months.

Remember, you're in this for the long haul. Don't bash your head against something for too long. If you become very frustrated or discouraged, go back to a slower tempo and play it a few times correctly before you quit. Go slowly enough that it's easy to play; increase speed only gradually. If you're making mistakes, you might be trying to play faster than you are yet capable of. Slow down and enjoy the ride!

The Recording Tells No Lies

Listening to yourself play an instrument on a recording is a lot like listening to your *voice* on a recording. It doesn't sound anything like what you thought it sounded like. Every little wobble and flub and mistake is painfully obvious. Again, we learn the most from making mistakes. But as with the metronome, don't let those mistakes stand. Fix 'em. Try recording yourself. You'll be surprised, and you might like doing it. You will definitely improve!

You Can Tune a Trumpet, but You Can't Tuna Fish

A *tuner* is a valuable tool. You will use a tuner to make sure your trumpet is generally in tune, and also to check all the notes on your trumpet to see whether *they* are in tune. For all the grimy details about notes that are out of tune on trumpets, see chapter 10, *Trumpet Tuning Tips.*

OTHER WAYS TO PLAY

You aren't limited to playing only during your daily session. There are opportunities throughout the day to hone your skills, and you don't even need your instrument. There's always buzzing exercises.

When I learn scales (there are hundreds of them and always more to work on), I practice the fingerings when away from the horn. To practice fingerings, you can get a set of valves from an instrument at the pawn shop and carry that around instead of the whole instrument; or simply do fingerings on your thumb or palm.

These are just a few suggestions. Use your noggin to think up some other options. There is a lot of "down" time in a day that you can use to improve your playing.

THE PRACTICE SESSION DETAILS

Warm-up: Mouthpiece Buzz

Of course, you've already checked to make sure your horn's working properly; you've got your music, metronome, recording equipment, and anything else you'll be using for this session. We'll start with buzzing. Use the CD to hear what this sounds like. We'll discuss how to read music in the next chapter.

> *8vb* means the note written sounds one octave (12 half steps) lower. *8va* means one octave higher.

glissando buzz: Buzz close to the pitches shown. Keep the sound full and constant as you slide up and down. Pay attention to dynamics. Do this exercise with a full, fat sound until there are no gaps or stops in the sound throughout the range. Repeat the exercise four or five times at a slightly lower pitch each time.

To improve your sound even more, buzz the following exercises with the same fat, full sound and check the pitches with the piano if you have access to one.

Warm-up: with the Horn

Once you've got a solid mouthpiece buzz, slide the mouthpiece firmly into your horn and play the following. If you're a beginner, some of these low notes may be a little difficult. Stay loose, use warm air, and keep the airflow steady. If the notes don't sound right away, keep at it until they do. For information about tonguing (separating the notes), see "Use My Tongue for What?" on page 48. For information on music reading, see chapter 6.

Here are warm-up exercises to help with tonguing and lip response. Keep the tempo slow at first. Once the notes are memorized, try the exercise at different speeds from slow to fast.

Repeat until airflow is smooth and all notes sound fat and full and fingers are limber. Vary the speed from slow to fast. Rhythmic precision is important. Fingerings are provided, but try to read the note and not the fingering.

If you have trouble getting the low notes in the previous exercise, try this variation. Fingering is the same. Repeat until airflow is smooth and all notes sound fat and full and fingers are limber.

The Exercises

There are so many things to work on that it's more than a little intimidating to think about, let alone tackle on the horn, but if you chip away at problem areas every day, you'll be a master trumpet player in a relatively short time. Your teacher will help you wade through the material and help you focus on what you need to work on most. Be persistent! Practice with intelligence and a critical ear.

There are so many exercises that there isn't space to include them all here—you'll have to get them from other books. The more the merrier. You'll have these books for life, or longer. I've been playing for over 25 years and still use many books, and buy more all the time. Start digging in!

The Fun Stuff

This section of your session is where you get to play actual songs. What a concept! Like the exercises, there are so many options here that it's hard to know where to start, because your ability constrains the choices of songs you would most benefit from. Your teacher will help you to become more aware of this.

Forget Written Music and Use Your Ear

Remember that music is *not* about notes on the page, but *is* about sounds and the emotions that those sounds can evoke. Take time during this part of your practice session to play along with a favorite song or piece of music so you can train your ear-finger-lip coordination. But beware! This is easy to say, and not as easy to put into practice. You'll have to play the song you choose over and over and over again, and each time you go at it, you'll figure out a little bit more of the song. As your ear becomes sharper, this will take less time.

MISTAKES AND HOW TO DEAL WITH THEM

When you practice, because you're pushing yourself, you are going to make mistakes. What's important is not that you made a mistake, but how you deal with the information. A mistake indicates a place where your abilities are not what they could be. What will you do with this information? Many of us simply ignore our mistakes because it shows us where we are lacking, and few of us are strong enough to really, truly face our shortcomings. That's too bad, because as far as trumpet playing goes, mistakes are pretty easy to fix. You've just got to do it.

PRACTICE AWARENESS

Playing correctly is more about awareness than just about anything. Often a student will play a simple passage that is well within their ability, yet they mess it up. When this happens, I point out that the phrase just missed is not difficult and not beyond the student's skill. Then I have them play it again.

Often, on the second repetition, the phrase is correct and much more beautiful. This is the point where I ask the question, "What was different about that time through the phrase?" Often the student doesn't know, so I ask "Are your skills suddenly better?" They shake their heads, no. "Have you acquired some special ability you didn't have the first time you played the phrase?" Again, most students shake their heads, no.

Finally, the student realizes that what is different is their awareness, their concentration level, and their focus. This is often a "light bulb" experience for many students. Playing music beautifully at your current skill level is more about awareness and focus than anything else. How aware are you? How intently can you focus on what you're doing?

Learning how to practice is one of the most important things to perfect. Without a decent approach to practice, your road to improvement may become a dead end. Persistence is your very best friend; improvement in *any* skill is often very gradual and ongoing. Stick with it!

Getting into It

CHAPTER 6

READING AND WRITING, BUT NO 'RITHMETIC

The notes I handle no better than many... But the pauses between the notes—ah, that is where the art resides.

—Arthur Schnabel (1882–1951)

What's Ahead:

- Basic note-reading skills
- Find your starting note
- C and G
- The first 5 notes of the C scale
- C scale variation
- The C blues scale

Terms to Know:

staff: The five lines and four spaces on which music is written.

ledger lines: Small lines used above and below the staff to extend its range.

A, B, C, D, E, F, G: The letters used to name musical pitches.

treble clef: A symbol at the beginning of the staff that sets the letter staff ($\oint$).

open: No valves pressed down.

fermata: A musical symbol indicating a hold or a pause ($\frown$).

stepwise: Moving from one note to the next available note up or down. Also known as *diatonic*.

WARNING: TAKE YOUR TIME!

If reading music is new to you, it will take some time before it makes sense. Refer back to this chapter as often as you need to. Just like anything else, mastery of written music can be a lifelong endeavor. Check out other books, Web sites, and teachers to learn more.

While learning about written music, continue to mess around with the trumpet. You'll be able to play things naturally that would seem very difficult if you had to read the musical notation. For example, play an open note (no valves down) and then fan your second valve (that means push it up and down as fast as you can). This is called a *trill*. It sounds cool and is easy to do. However, the notation for a trill isn't taught in any beginning trumpet book or band method that I know of. To find out about more of these devices, see chapter 15, *Trumpet Sound Effects*.

AN ULTRA-BRIEF INTRO TO WRITTEN MUSIC

If you've never read music before, prepare to be a little bewildered by the information and terms I'm about to throw at you. Don't panic! You only have to remember one or two concepts for now. For more information and clear explanations, pick up a copy of *Basic Music Theory: How to Read, Write, and Understand Written Music*.

The Staff

Music is written on a *staff* (plural *staves*), which is five horizontal parallel lines. The five lines create four spaces between them. Lines and spaces are numbered from the bottom to the top.

Names of the Notes

You only need the first seven letters of the alphabet for written music. The music alphabet uses A, B, C, D, E, F, and G. You'll never find an "H" in music, or a "Q", or anything other than A through G. Below you can see the letter names of each staff line.

When notes go higher or lower than the staff, *ledger lines* (also spelled *leger*) are used to extend the staff. Next are examples of trumpet ledger line notes below the staff. Ledger lines also occur above the staff, but you won't have to worry about them yet.

Here are leger line notes above and below the staff. You'll rarely go lower or higher than these notes.

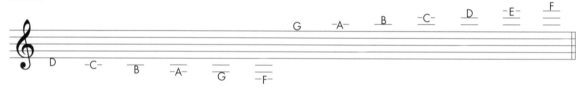

You Got Rhythm

There are only three different note lengths to learn at first. You'll notice that the half notes and quarter notes have two examples, one with the stem down (high notes on the staff) and one with the stem up (notes low on the staff).

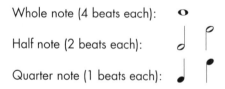

The Rests of the Story

Silence in music is as important as sound. Rest names and lengths are the same as the note lengths you learned above. They are *whole rests, half rests,* and *quarter rests.*

Whole rests hang from the fourth line, are four beats long, and look like this:

Half rests sit on the third line, are two beats long, and look like this:

Quarter rests are one beat long, sit smack in the middle of the staff, and look like this:

Quarter Rest

Whole rests and half rests look very much the same and can be easily confused with each other. Here's a way to remember which is which. The whole rest, looks like a *hole* in the ground. The half rest looks a little bit like a *hat* (I know, *half* and *hat* don't sound the same, but work with me here).

C AND G: YOUR FIRST WRITTEN NOTES

Your first *written* notes—you've probably played many by now that are not written down—are fingered "open" (no valves down). You may find one of these easier to play than the other. The upper one is named "G" and the lower one is "C."

The "C" is the lowest open note on the trumpet and is usually the easiest note for beginners to play. For some, however, the "G" comes out more easily. Try to play both. To find out if you've got the right notes you can check the track on the CD, play the note on a piano, or have your teacher help you.

If you already know the notes on the piano keyboard you'll notice that the notes you see written on the keyboard are not the correct names for the notes on the piano. Don't worry. Trumpet is what's called a B-flat instrument, and this means its notes are different from those on piano, which is a C instrument. Don't sweat it right now if that seems confusing (and it is confusing). To learn more about this, see chapter 17, *The Transposing Trumpeter.*

These are your first written notes on trumpet. The notes are shown as whole notes (four beats) but play them for as long as you can.

You can see on the keyboard that there are six other notes between G and C. There are also six other valve combinations between the open notes you just learned. Can you discover what they are without the fingering chart in the back of the book? You'll remember them better if you work it out for yourself (Hint: second valve changes pitch a half step, first valve changes pitch a whole step, and third valve changes pitch a step and a half). We won't deal with all six combinations just yet. Practice the C and the G until you can get them both easily and can hear/feel the difference between the two.

MORE NOTES: D, E, AND F

Although there are six notes between G and C, you'll only need three of them for a while. The three notes are D, E, and F.

Here are D, E, and F as whole notes side by side with fingering. Check your pitches with a piano or keyboard or with the CD.

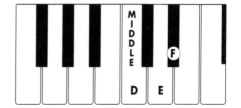

I'll say this many times in the hopes that it will stick: Music is not about notes on the page, but it is about sound. Don't worry about getting the right number of beats per note in the examples below. Simply hold out each note with the most beautiful tone you can muster for one full breath, then go on to the next.

Memorize these notes as quickly as possible, both in the way they sound and how they feel to play. Practice them forwards and backwards and in as many combinations as possible. Invent songs with these notes.

If one of your goals is to learn how to read music, glance at the fingering if necessary, then focus on the written note. If you stare at the fingering, *that* is what you'll learn. When it comes time to read the notes without fingerings you'll be lost because you memorized the fingering and not the note.

Here are the first five notes of the trumpet's C major scale in various order. Play any other combination you can come up with. Hold each note for one full breath.

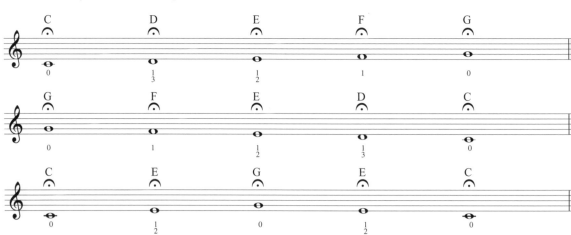

Below are some examples with skips between notes. Play any other combination you can come up with. Hold each note for one full breath.

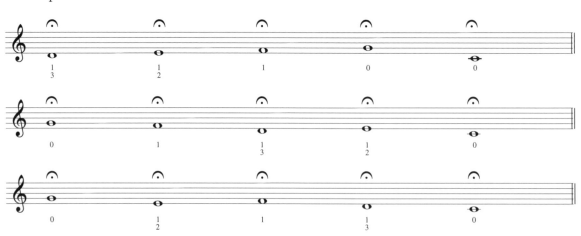

Once you have these five notes memorized, begin to vary the speed and the order in which you play them. Tap your foot to keep it rhythmic and use a metronome to keep yourself steady. Tips about how to use the metronome are in chapter 5.

The *time signature* (the ⁴⁄₄ symbol at the start of the example below) is a way to tell musicians about the music they are reading. The top number tells you how many beats are in one measure. The bottom number tells you what kind of note gets one beat. Most examples are in 4/4 time: Four beats per measure and the quarter notes gets one beat.

READING THE MUSIC

Now you'll add rhythm to the notes you've learned. Tap your foot or use a metronome to help get the count right on all the notes and rests. Rests are placed to give you a chance to prepare for the next note. Look ahead, push the right valves, and get your chops ready so you can play exactly on the first beat of the next measure.

Read the notes and not the fingerings. Tap your foot. Whole notes and whole rests get four beats.

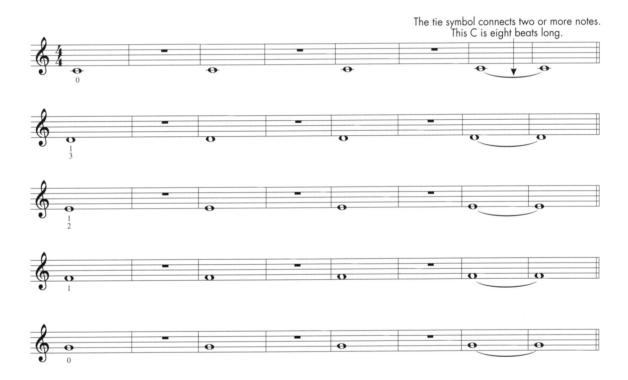

Changing Notes

The previous exercises were about as simple as written music can get. The next exercises are a little more difficult, but are still pretty simple. Look ahead and change fingerings during the rests. I've included the fingerings for these first exercises, but by now you should have the fingering memorized for each note. If they're not memorized yet, you've got your first project to work on.

On the following page are whole notes and whole rests. Tap your foot to be sure each gets four beats. Look ahead so you can change fingerings during the rest. Listen to the CD if you need help.

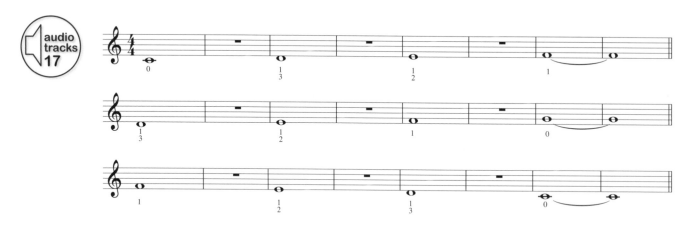

Most of the examples before this have been *stepwise*, or *diatonic*, which means they move from one note to the next line or space note higher or lower. In the examples below, there are skips between notes, so read ahead during the rest to be ready. Try to hear the note before you play it.

Set the tongue and use the air to blast it open when you say "too." When the air and tongue are coordinated, notes sound cleanly and clearly. You'll get more tongue tips in the next chapter.

Read ahead so you're ready for the note change. Listen to the CD if you need help.

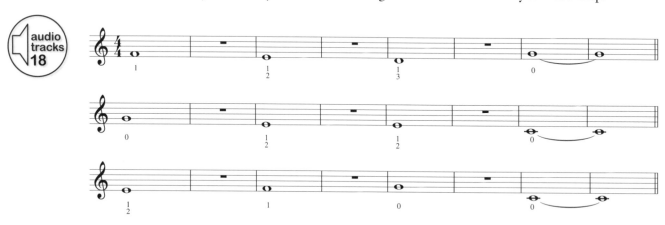

MORE NOTES!

If you've got those first five notes memorized, move on to the notes below. Just as with the first notes you learned, play these for one full breath and focus in on the quality of your tone. Play them many times until you have the feel and sound and fingering of the note memorized. Make up your own songs using these notes.

Use the C you already know to get your ears working, then try for the lower notes. Use warm, slow air, like you're making steam come from your mouth on a cold day. If you need help, play along with the CD or ask a teacher.

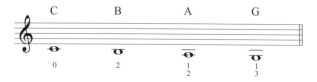

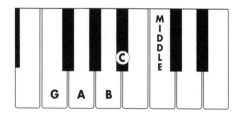

PLAYING HIGHER: NOTES ABOVE G

Playing higher takes air support, correct embouchure formation, good posture, and some chop strength. If you've been doing your buzzing both with lips only and with the mouthpiece, you'll probably have no trouble with the following notes.

Take large breaths because higher notes need faster air. The only way to get your air faster is to take more of it into your lungs and compress it before blowing. Don't use excessive pressure on your lips to get these notes! For more information on increasing your range, see chapter 12, *Home on the High Range*.

If you get these notes easily and want to learn more, check out the fingering chart in the back of the book and get yourself a song book that uses notes higher in the range. Good job, keep it up!

The A, B, and C are above the second line G. If you need help, play along with the CD.

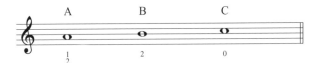
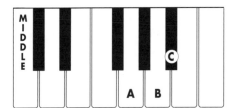

You have probably noticed that we've begun to repeat some note names, like C, A, and B. Remember there are only seven letter names for notes in music. As you go higher, note names repeat at the *octave*, or every eight notes.

Sources for Further Study

Think about how long it took you to learn how to read English and how much you had to study in order to do it. Learning to read written music is not as difficult as learning to read words, but it will take some time and effort. Here are some sources to help you on your way.

- *Basic Music Theory: How to Read, Write, and Understand Written Music*, by Jonathan Harnum (www.sol-ut.com)
- *Music Theory*, by Barrett Tagliarino (Hal Leonard)

CHAPTER 7

TONGUE TIPS FOR TRUMPET

While thou livest keep a good tongue in thy head.

—William Shakespeare (1564–1616)

What's Ahead:
- Why tongue?
- Basic tonguing
- Double tonguing
- Triple tonguing

Terms to Know:

articulation: The use of the tongue in a wind instrument to separate notes in various ways.

legato: Smooth and connected. Shown by a line (−) above or below notes.

slur: No tonguing. Notes are connected with the air stream only.

staccato: Short and detached. Shown by a dot (·) above or below the note.

double-tonguing: Using the "t" and "k" to articulate music that is too fast for single-tonguing (using just the "t").

dorsal tonguing: A style of tonguing in which the middle of the tongue strikes the roof of the mouth (say "goo-goo-ga-ga" and you've done it).

USE MY TONGUE FOR WHAT?

The tongue plays an essential role in trumpet music; it allows you to separate notes cleanly and clearly. It will also help you play higher, and with it you can do some cool sound effects. You'll learn about all the details of tonguing in this chapter. Be aware that some of these techniques, like double and triple tonguing, will take a lot of practice to master.

The tongue is one of the strangest muscles in the body. Unlike most others, it's only attached at one end. Like any muscle, the tongue can be trained to be quicker, stronger, and more limber.

Articulation is a generic word for different types of tonguing. In a slow, sweet song, the articulation would be smooth and light with notes connected, also known as *legato*. In a march, the articulation would be shorter, more forceful, and with the notes separated, or *marcato*. Very short notes are called *staccato*. In a jazz band or a rock 'n' roll horn section, you'd use another kind of articulation. The cool thing is that no matter what style of music you end up playing, use of the tongue is crucial to get the kind of sound you need.

BASIC TONGUING

The only hard and fast rule about tonguing is that when you do it, whichever style you're using, don't let your jaw move *at all*. If you jaw moves, this can throw off your embouchure and your airstream and will cause more difficulties than you want. Keep your jaw still. In the beginning it's a good idea to practice in front of a mirror to make sure your jaw isn't moving.

If you can say, "too", then you've got the essence of tonguing down already. Say "tah" and "too" and "tee" a few times and feel where your tongue hits inside your mouth. The tip of your tongue usually touches behind your teeth, right where your gums and teeth come together. If you use the "tah" syllable, be sure your jaw doesn't drop when the "ah" sound comes out. Use a mirror or put a hand on your jaw to be sure.

There are other ways to tongue besides using syllables that start with "t." Try using a "doo" sound. Compare where your tongue hits when you use this syllable. It should strike your soft palate; that flat part just back from your teeth. Also try "thoo" or "the", with the tongue touching the bottom edge of the top teeth. Other options are "ka" and "la." Try these and other syllables and see what sounds you create.

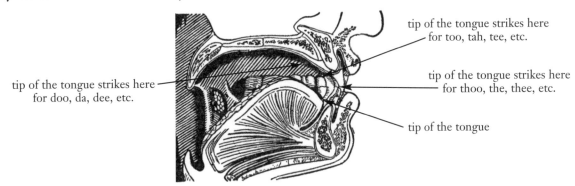

tip of the tongue strikes here for too, tah, tee, etc.

tip of the tongue strikes here for thoo, the, thee, etc.

tip of the tongue strikes here for doo, da, dee, etc.

tip of the tongue

In classical music you often want the cleanest, clearest articulations possible, so the "t" or "th" syllables are best for this. In jazz, often the softer articulations are preferred, like a "dah" or "doo" tonguing. Try them all and use the one you like best. It's a good idea to be able to do *any* kind of tonguing, so learn 'em all and you'll have more options.

THE AIRSTREAM AND THE TONGUE

Imagine you're holding a garden hose turned on full blast. The water streams out of the hose in a solid arc across the grass. Quickly chop your hand back and forth through the stream of water. As the water arcs out over the grass, the stream is chopped into small chunks even though the flow of water is constant.

Do you get the analogy? Your airstream is the water and your tongue is the hand breaking the stream into small chunks. It's *VERY IMPORTANT* to keep that airstream going, just like the flow of water in the hose. The airstream is what gives your sound power, strength, and range, and allows you to change cleanly from one note to the next. Without a strong steady airstream, your sound will not be full and present and it will be more difficult to be consistent.

Play the following exercises. *Keep the air moving* through the tongue strike. With the third and fourth exercises, gradually speed up until your tongue gives out. Buzz these both with your chops alone and with the mouthpiece.

don't forget

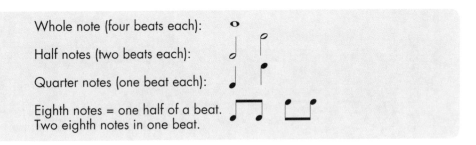

Whole note (four beats each):

Half notes (two beats each):

Quarter notes (one beat each):

Eighth notes = one half of a beat.
Two eighth notes in one beat.

Repeat Signs

A *repeat sign* is two dots at the end of a section of music and these dots tell you to go back and repeat the previous section. Sometimes the repeat will be back to the beginning, and sometimes a section in the middle of a song will be repeated. When a middle section is repeated, return to the previous repeat sign.

Breathe deeply. Don't stop the air between notes! When you need a breath, especially with the eighth notes, take a quick one so the rhythm isn't interrupted. Repeat several times. Eighth notes are explained in more detail on page 62. For now, you can use the CD to hear and feel the eighth-note rhythm.

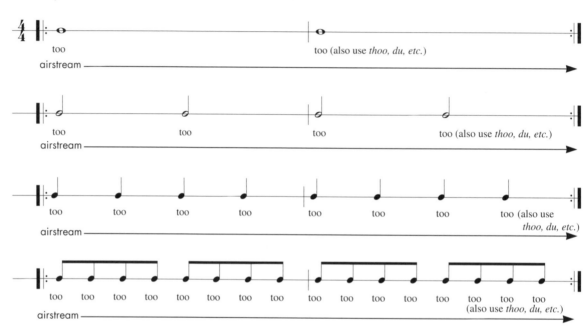

Here are some more suggestions for tonguing on the horn. Keep the airflow steady and strike swiftly with the tip of the tongue.

Breathe deeply. Don't stop the air between notes! Repeat several times. Coordinate your tongue and finger movements. Notice that the last line is in 2/4 meter. This means two beats per measure and the quarter note gets the beat.

It's important that your fingers and tongue start notes together. This is pretty easy when playing music like you've had so far. As notes go by more quickly it's important to finger and tongue them at the same time. Try doing it right now, since your tongue is already warmed up. Pick two or three notes with different fingerings and tongue back and forth between them. How fast can you do it cleanly?

THE TONGUE'S ROLE IN PLAYING HIGH AND LOW

Be aware of your tongue for a few moments. Say "ahh" and feel where your tongue is in your mouth. Now say "eee" and feel what happens with your tongue. The back of your tongue is down during the "ahh" sound and it rises toward the roof of your mouth for the "eee" sound.

When you use these syllables while playing, it's natural for your jaw to drop down for the "ahh" sound and rise for the "eee" sound. This is great if you're talking, but bad if you're playing. Moving the jaw will make things more difficult for you. Keep your jaw still while doing the following. If you don't have a mirror, put a hand on your jaw to monitor it.

Keep your mouth closed with your teeth slightly apart as though you were going to play trumpet. Keep your jaw relaxed but don't move it as you do the following. Silently say "ahh" then "eee" again and feel how your tongue moves. Go back and forth between the two very slowly at first (it would sound like aahhhhhhheeeeeeeeeee). Do this several times until you've got a good feel for it. Now do it quickly so your tongue snaps back and forth between the lower and upper position. Do this in a mirror or with a hand on your jaw to make sure your jaw doesn't move.

Now you'll add the buzz. Buzz a low note and use the "ahh" shape with your tongue. Make the pitch go higher gradually and as you do, change from the "ahh" shape to the "eee" shape. Do this several times. Then make an abrupt switch from low (ahh) to high (eee) and be sure your jaw doesn't move.

It may be difficult to coordinate at first but keep trying. You'll need this skill, so practice it until you've got it. Practice with a mirror or with a hand on your jaw to be sure your jaw doesn't move. Add the mouthpiece and do the same thing as above. It's said that it takes seven repetitions before something sticks in our head. Don't move your jaw!

Remember it's more difficult to go from low to high than it is from high to low. Don't move your jaw!

Tonguing: Low, Middle, High

Studies have shown that tongue placement depends on where in the trumpet's range you're playing. When playing low, the tongue strikes between the teeth, and in some cases, even all the way up to the lips. As you go higher, the tongue moves further back behind the teeth. For very high playing the tongue moves back even further, often striking the soft palate behind the upper teeth. For altissimo playing (very high), many players use *dorsal tonguing*, where the *middle* of the tongue strikes the roof of the mouth. Experiment with your own tongue to see which placement works best for you.

Tongue Use in Lip Slurs

A slur is moving from one note to another without tonguing, as smoothly as possible. All wind instruments use slurs, which are shown by a curved line connecting the notes. Trumpet players have an added challenge when the slur is between two notes with the same fingering, like between the open notes G and C. A slur between two notes which share the same fingering is called a *lip slur*.

Because they're a little tricky and because they're important, lip slurs get their own chapter. You won't have long to wait because lip slurs are covered in the next chapter.

The Oral Cavity's Role in Tone Quality

If all the above wasn't enough, the tongue affects the size of the oral cavity, and this affects your tone quality. If your tongue is up high in your mouth (small oral cavity) your tone will be less rich and warm than it could be. With your tongue down low (ahhh) and an open throat (large oral cavity), your tone will be richer and more resonant. Think of the difference between a little acoustic guitar with a small resonating chamber and a jumbo dreadnought-size acoustic guitar. The bigger guitar will have a larger, more resonant, and more pleasing tone.

Remember the breathing tube from the chapter on breathing? When you use the breathing tube, it forces your tongue down and makes your throat open up, giving you the largest oral cavity you can have. If you play with the inside of your mouth very open like this, your tone will be more resonant and pleasing. The trouble with using a very open oral cavity is that it becomes more difficult to play in the upper range. You have to compromise. Keep your oral cavity as large as you can without sacrificing range.

DOUBLE- AND TRIPLE-TONGUING

At times you may have to play a passage that is very fast—too fast to tongue in the usual manner (also called "single-tonguing"). In such cases, you'll want to use double, or triple tonguing. This is an advanced skill that is not difficult at all to understand, but it will take a while before it becomes natural and easy.

Your tongue is a muscle and will tire easily at first and might seem slow and stubborn. The more you train your tongue, the quicker and stronger it will become. Many of these exercises you can do anywhere, but you might want to do them silently so people don't give you strange looks.

These techniques use both the front part of the tongue (the tah, too, tee, the, or thoo sound) and the back part of the tongue (the kah or koo or kee sound). Take a moment and say, "ka, ka, ka, ka," and feel where your tongue strikes.

don't forget

As before, you don't want your jaw to move for all the same reasons. Practice with a mirror or a hand on your jaw.

Double-Tonguing

Do the following very slowly! Combine the two syllables you learned above and say, "tee-kee-tee-kee-tee-kee," and "too-koo-too-koo-too-koo," and "tah-kah-tah-kah-tah-kah." Go slowly and keep a hand on your jaw. Keep the length of each syllable even.

Use a metronome with the following exercises and find a tempo at which you can say the syllables easily. START SLOWLY! On the third exercise, gradually speed up a few metronome clicks with each repetition. See how fast you can go before your tongue gives out. Rest a few minutes, then do it again. Monitor yourself like this so you can see how much better you're getting. Charts to keep track of this can be found at www.sol-ut.com. Do this daily and you'll have a fast tongue in a short time.

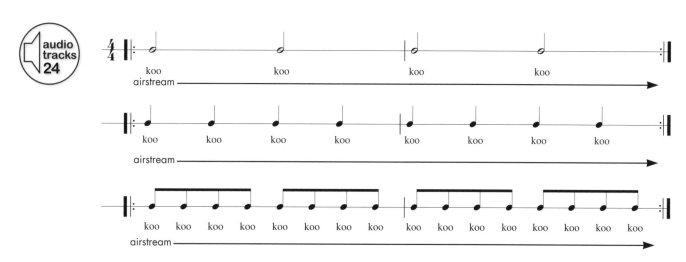

Now you'll do double-tonguing with the buzz and the mouthpiece. These exercises have the same rhythm as above, but the syllables alternate. Strive to make the "too" and "koo" sound *exactly* the same. This is one of the challenging parts of double-tonguing.

Also use the tah-kah and tee-kee syllables in these next exercises. Keep the air moving! Do these both with and without the mouthpiece.

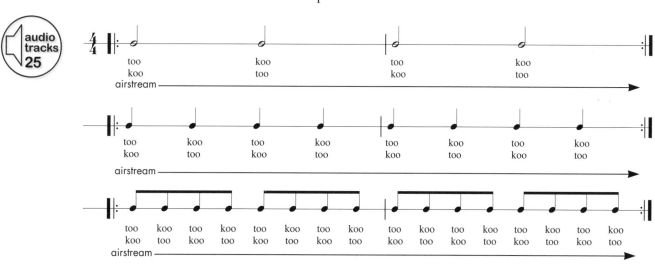

When you add the horn to your double-tonguing, you'll be able to hear very clearly the difference between using the tip of the tongue ("too") and the back of the tongue ("koo"). Strive to make the two sound exactly the same by making that "koo" syllable hard and explosive. As before, keep the air flowing and keep your jaw still.

Triple-Tonguing

There isn't much difference between double- and triple-tonguing technique. You'll still use the "ta" and "ka" syllables (or too-koo, etc.). The rhythm of the notes will be different (usually triplets) and depending on which type of triple-tonguing you choose, the order may also be slightly different.

You have two options for triple-tonguing. The first is to use the double-tonguing pattern you already learned, but to group it in threes. That would sound like "**ta**-ka-ta, **ka**-ta-ka, **ta**-ka-ta, **ka**-

ta-ka," etc. Notice that each group of three alternates the first syllable. It is this alternation which makes this method a challenge. Give it a try and see how you like it.

Another way of triple-tonguing is to use the pattern "ta-ka-ta, ta-ka-ta, ta-ka-ta," etc. Try this method of triple-tonguing and see how it feels compared to the first technique, then focus on one until it's learned.

Listen to Colin Oldberg demonstrate triple-tonguing in an excerpt from *Scheherazade* by Rimsky-Korsakov.

The following are triple-tonguing exercises to buzz. Notice the different time signatures. START SLOWLY! With the third example, gradually speed up with your metronome until your tongue gives out. Rest a few minutes, then do it again. The rhythms in the third example are called *triplets*, which are three eighth notes evenly spaced within one beat. Listen to the CD to get a feel for the triplet rhythm.

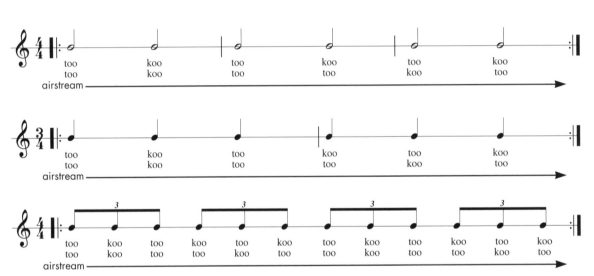

Accidentals on Purpose

Accidentals change the pitch of a note slightly (a half step). A flat lowers the pitch a half step, a sharp raises the pitch a half step, and a natural sign cancels the effects of a flat or sharp.

An accidental affects the entire measure. Notes after the initial accidental in the same measure are also affected and use the same fingering.

Now try it with the horn. Practice variations of the following exercises on every note in your range.

Track 28
(0:34)

Multiple Tonguing While Changing Notes

Once you've practiced multiple tonguing on one note, it's time to practice multiple tonguing while changing notes. This is a little more challenging, but if you've got the basics down it's not that hard to make the leap to double- or triple-tonguing melodically.

The challenge lies in coordinating the tongue and the fingers. As with any coordination challenge, you have to start *very slowly* to train the muscles to perform the movement correctly. Get it perfect at a slow tempo (use your metronome) and then gradually speed it up. It's that simple, you just have to do it.

Here are double- and triple-tonguing exercises. START SLOWLY! With the third example, gradually speed up with your metronome until your tongue gives out. Rest a few minutes, then do it again. Do this daily and you'll have a fast tongue in a short time.

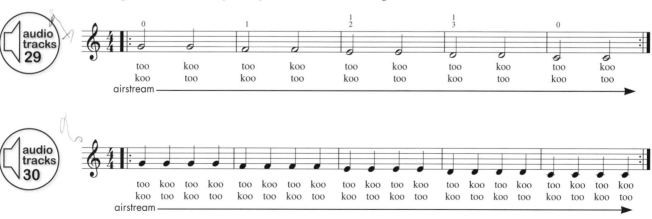

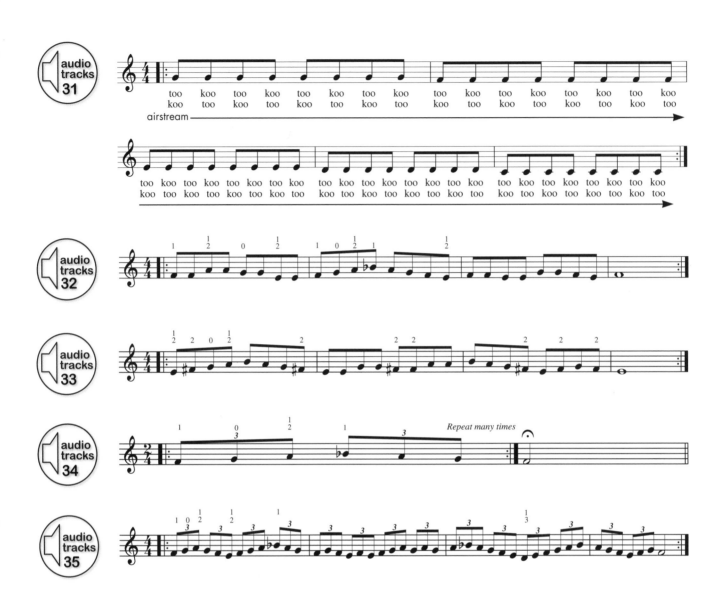

Sources for Further Study

If you don't have an *Arban's Complete Method for Trumpet*, go get one now. It has exercises for most techniques on trumpet, including many double- and triple-tonguing exercises.

Some great recordings of double- and triple-tonguing can be found on Wynton Marsalis's album *Carnival*, especially "Flight of the Bumblebee." Also find further examples in *Scheherazade*, by Rimsky-Korsakov, in Tchaikovsky's Symphony IV, the third movement of Hummel's Concerto in E♭, and many, many others.

CHAPTER 8
LIP SLURS AND THE ORAL CAVITY

Smile—it's the second best thing you can do with your lips.

—Anonymous

What's Ahead:

- Regular slur
- What is a lip slur?
- Lip slur techniques
- Lip slur exercises
- Lip slur method books

Terms to know:

lip slur: The technique of moving from one note to another using the same fingering without the use of the tongue.

oral cavity: The space inside your mouth and throat. Used to affect the sound you get on the horn.

WHAT IS A LIP SLUR?

On a wind instrument, a regular slur is two different notes smoothly connected using the air alone, no tonguing. This is usually an easy skill, but with brass instruments like trumpet, many notes share the same fingering. When one note of a slur shares the fingering with the next note of the slur, the change has to be made with the chops and the airstream alone. This is called a *lip slur*.

In a regular slur, like the first example below, fingerings are different from one note to the next: Notice the fingerings change for each note.

Some lip slurs involve changing between notes with the same fingering without using the tongue. Here is an example. There is one regular slur in this example. Can you spot it? Notice the fingerings don't change for all but one note.

Track 36
(0:10)

Experiment with lip slurs to get a feel for what you can and can't do. Choose a valve combination and see how many notes you can get on that combination without using your tongue to change notes. Keep the air steady. Trying to figure out for yourself how to do lip slurs will help you understand what you need to learn.

Lip slurs are essential to playing trumpet. As you practice them you'll be increasing your flexibility and dexterity. Lip slurs keep lips limber. Practice them regularly.

LIP SLURS AND PHYSICS: DOWNHILL IS EASIER

Is it easier to go uphill or downhill? Does it take more work to climb a cliff or fall off one? Descending lip slurs are easier. Going from a high energy state (higher note) to a lower energy state (low note) requires no extra energy.

For our example we'll use G and C, your first two notes. Play the G and be aware of how it feels: how hard you have to blow, the tension of your chops, the sound of the note. Then play the C and do the same thing. Notice the differences between notes. You'll do this for each of the examples below, too. It will help a lot when you do the actual slur.

If the higher note just won't drop down, try mouthing the word "ahhh" as you change notes, but don't let your jaw move. To do this you must change the shape formed by the inside of your mouth, the oral cavity.

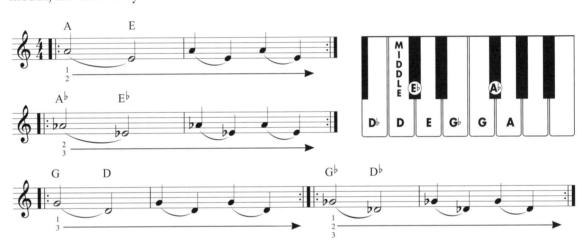

The next lip slurs have a greater distance between them, so you may find them a little more challenging. As you go to the low note, use warm, slower air, like you're saying, "Haaahhhhh."

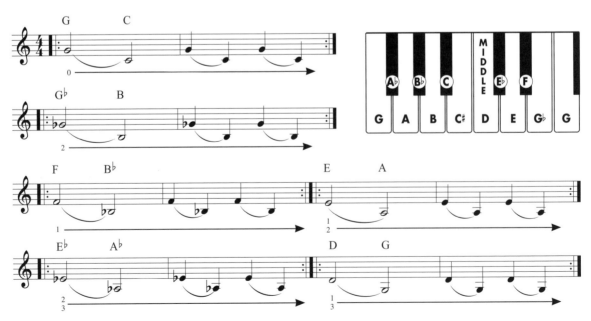

GOING UP!

An ascending, or rising lip slur is more difficult, but there are some things you can do to help. A lip slur from low to high requires extra energy. The important energy source to rely on is your airstream. As you do a lip slur from a lower note, give the airstream a push to change to the upper note. Think of blowing a fly away with a puff of air, or blowing dust off something: a quick pulse of air. Experiment with just how much air it will take to get results. In addition to the airstream, you can change the shape of the inside of your mouth (oral cavity) to get the higher note of the lip slur.

This oral cavity is not something you'll need filled by a dentist. It's the shape of the inside of your mouth and throat. The size of the oral cavity is changed by your tongue. Do this: without opening your lips or moving your jaw, mouth the word "ahhh" and be aware of where your tongue is. And again without opening your lips or moving your jaw, mouth the word "eeee" and feel where your tongue is. Finally, still with closed lips and stationary jaw, mouth "ahhh" and then "eeee" and feel the position of your tongue change. You've just changed the size and shape of your oral cavity with your tongue position. Not too difficult, is it? If you know how to whistle, you can already do this.

Raising the tongue speeds up the airstream. It is the airspeed that allows you to play higher.

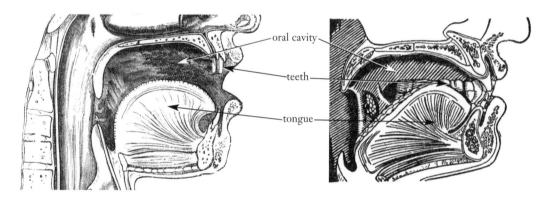

When you go from "ahh" to "eee" don't move your embouchure, jaw, and lips, unlike the drawings above.

Tongue the half notes and be aware of how each note feels. When you slur from the lower note to the higher, make your airstream faster, as though you're blowing out a candle. Use the "ahhh-to-eee" technique if you can't get the note to change with the airstream alone. Go slowly. Check your pitch with a piano or with the CD.

It will be tempting to use mouthpiece pressure to get to that upper note. Don't do it! Use the airstream and tongue position only. It will take some time and effort to master this skill and it's best to start with the smallest jumps between notes, like the following examples.

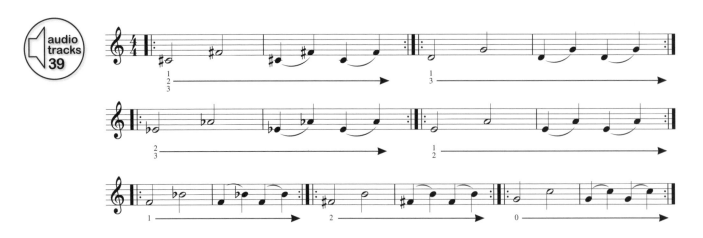

Once you have a handle on small skips, try some bigger skips, like the ones below:

LARGE-INTERVAL LIP SLURS

Sometimes it's necessary to do a lip slur between notes that are far apart. Because there are other notes with the same fingering between the two notes of the big slur, the challenge is to get the slur smooth without any of the notes in the middle. Confused? Here's an example:

Try the octave slur from high to low first. Between the two Cs there is a G on the second line which shares the open fingering. The challenge is to get from one C to another without the G sounding. Blow through the notes. Listen to the CD and keep trying until you can get it.

The airstream is even more important for these big leaps. Keep your airflow steady and blow through the notes so the horn does the work. Keep practicing. Talk to your trumpet teacher about lip slurs.

TUNES FROM SIMPLE TO SOPHISTICATED

Do not follow in the footsteps of the wise. Seek what they sought.
—Zen saying

What's Ahead:

- Eighth notes
- Flats
- Minor
- E♭ and A♭

Terms to know:

repeat sign: Two dots at the end of a section telling you to repeat the section.

breath mark: A comma-shaped symbol telling you to take a breath.

upbeat: The second half of a beat (the second of two eighth notes).

round: A song in which the same melody is played by all players starting in different places.

flat (♭): A symbol used to lower the pitch of a note by a half step.

sharp (♯): A symbol used to raise the pitch of a note by a half step.

natural (♮): A symbol used to cancel a flat or sharp.

lead sheet: Shorthand for the melody line, lyrics, chords, and outline of a song (also called a "chart").

The first tunes you'll see are those that most musicians have played in the process of learning to read music. You might already know most of these melodies. Follow the notes and not the fingerings so you learn to read the music. On some tunes I didn't write the fingering under the notes so you'd be forced to remember the fingerings.

The first few songs are simple and this makes them easy to play, but the boredom potential is high. If you want to jump ahead to the tougher tunes, go for it! Use the CD to help you out.

BUZZ THESE TUNES!

If you've been playing for a while you may think these simple songs offer nothing for you, but that might not be true. Can you sing them perfectly in tune? Can you buzz them perfectly?

To challenge and strengthen your ability on trumpet, buzz all these little tunes with your mouthpiece. Start in a comfortable middle range and give it a try. If you need a little help, use a piano or your trumpet to get the right pitch in your ear. Once you're able to buzz all of these on your mouthpiece, buzz the tunes with just your lips. Buzz these tunes a couple times a day for a few weeks and you'll be rewarded with better tone, better range, better control of your sound, and better listening skills. Why wouldn't you want all that good stuff?

Mary Had a Little Lamb

Words by Sarah Josepha Hale
Traditional Music

Au Clair De La Lune

French Folksong

The following example is "Twinkle, Twinkle Little Star." The legend is that Mozart wrote this tune when he was five. Actually, he used the already-existing melody for a composition. Still pretty amazing.

Twinkle, Twinkle Little Star

Traditional

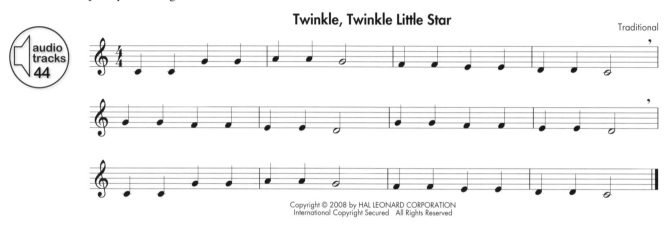

You probably know this next one. The rhythms shown are simpler than the tune you sing. Play it as you know it or as it's written. Try it both ways.

Jingle Bells

Words and Music by J. Pierpont

EIGHTH NOTES

When you tap your foot (you *are* tapping your foot, right?) the first of two eighth notes is played when your foot hits the floor and the second is played when your foot is in the "up" position. The second of two eighth notes is called the *upbeat* for this reason.

In common time (four-four: four beats per measure and the quarter note gets one beat) eighth notes are counted, "one-and-two-and-three-and-four-and." Before we get to songs with eighth notes, let's give you a little practice on some simple examples. This will give you a chance to coordinate your tongue and your foot.

Keep your foot tap steady and even. Go slowly enough to make it easy. Say the counting out loud while tapping your foot if you're having trouble coordinating the foot and the trumpet playing. There is a pause between each line.

Simple Tunes with Eighth Notes

Notice there are only two beats in each measure. The quarter note still gets one beat. Tap your foot at a steady tempo.

Hot Cross Buns

Traditional

Skip to My Lou

Traditional

AND NOW SOME TOUGHER (AND COOLER!) TUNES

I gave you the above tunes in the interest of simplicity because trumpet is difficult enough at the beginning without a lot of notes and tricky rhythms. However, it's *very important* to remember that making music is *not* about notes on a page, it's about sound and the emotion that sound can convey. If you're a good listener, you'll be able to play music that is much more difficult than you'd be able to read. In the following examples, if the written notes are too confusing, get the recording so you can hear what the tune sounds like, then use the fingerings to play along. *Making music is not necessarily about being able to read music!* That being said, however, learning to read is a good skill. One of the first steps towards mastery is associating notes with fingerings. Most of the examples below have fingerings written in, but some do not. You can write in the fingerings of these pieces or, better yet, memorize the fingerings.

Because you are only one musician (and a trumpeter to boot), the musical examples you'll see below are only a small part of the whole tune. Mostly I've just given you the melody or an important section in the tune. If you're interested in browsing supplemental material, such as scales to work on with these songs, rhythm-section parts, or links to the recordings, visit www.sol-ut.com.

Some of these tunes might be too high for you, so I've included a version one octave lower.

Clocks

Clocks
(8vb)

I've included a first and second ending in writing out this hook from Bob Marley's "Get Up, Stand Up" (*Songs of Freedom*, d.2). Follow the music to the repeat sign, play again from the beginning, and this second time you'll skip the first ending and go directly to the second ending.

Get Up, Stand Up

Swing, in the following song, means a lilting, bouncy kind of feel. Listen to the original tune and you'll hear Ringo swing while he sings.

Yellow Submarine

Words and Music by
John Lennon and Paul McCartney

This next tune is from an excellent album produced by Ry Cooder and features some incredible Cuban musicians, including Manuel Mirabal on trumpet. This trumpet part begins the song. Don't forget your straight mute. To learn more about mutes, see chapter 16.

Dos Gardenias

Words and Music by
Isolina Carillo

CLASSICAL MUSIC EXAMPLES

The above popular tunes you might be familiar with. There is a whole world of different musical styles available to you, from Africa to Asia to America and beyond. Below are some pieces of western classical music that are fairly easy, and a couple that are a challenge both rhythmically and because of their range. In the case of the three-part excerpts, if you're still working on your range, the lower parts will be easier for you. Listen to the CD. Find links to good recordings and classical excerpt books at www.sol-ut.com.

Sixteenth Notes: If you're good with fractions, you know that sixteenth notes are twice as fast as eighth notes. There are four sixteenth notes in one beat, and sixteen in a measure of common time. A counting system for sixteenth and other rhythms is included in the following example.

Here is a very popular request at classical trumpet auditions. This piece gives you an opportunity to practice your double-tonguing skills.

Leonore Overture No. 3

By Ludwig van Beethoven

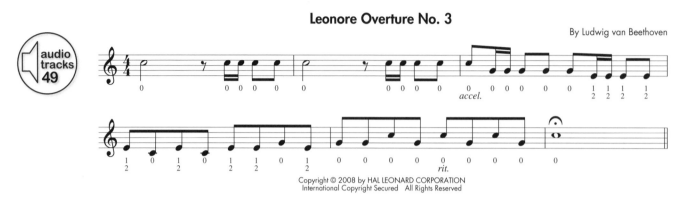

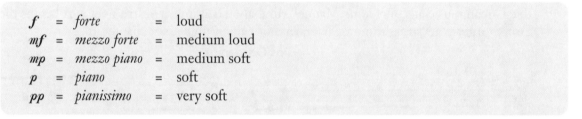

f = *forte*	=	loud
mf = *mezzo forte*	=	medium loud
mp = *mezzo piano*	=	medium soft
p = *piano*	=	soft
pp = *pianissimo*	=	very soft

This is also a common request in a classical audition. The nice thing about this excerpt is that you can play it with your friends. Or, if you aren't yet able to play the high part yet, play one of the lower parts along with the CD. Count carefully to keep your place during the changing time signatures.

Theme–Pictures at an Exhibition

By Modest Mussorgsky

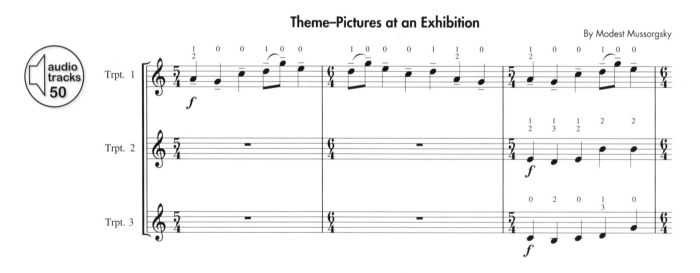

This is the opening statement of the popular trumpet concerto in E♭ by Johann Nepomuk Hummel. The "tr" symbol in the last system is a *trill*. See page 114 to learn more.

Trumpet Concerto in E♭ Major

By Johann Nepomuk Hummel

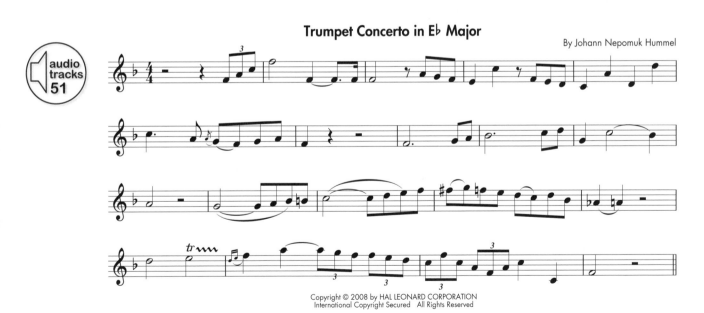

6/8 time: Six beats per measure and the eighth note gets one beat.

Following is one of the classic theme-and-variations cornet solos that has been played so well by so many. Listen to trumpet artists who have recorded this piece. The squiggly symbol in the second system is called a *turn*. See page 115 to learn more.

Carnival of Venice
Opening Statement

By Jean-Baptiste Arban

Here's another great trumpet excerpt that you can play along with the CD. As before, if your chops aren't up to the challenge of the first part, play a lower part. Colin, Jean, and Paul sound great on this small section of this four-movement symphony. Find a recording of the whole symphony at sol-ut.com. It's a great piece of music!

Symphony No. 5, Movement I (27–29)

Music by Dmitri Shostakovich

This next excerpt is one of Richard Wagner's most widely recognized pieces, from act III of the opera *Die Walküre*.

Ride of the Valkyries

By Richard Wagner

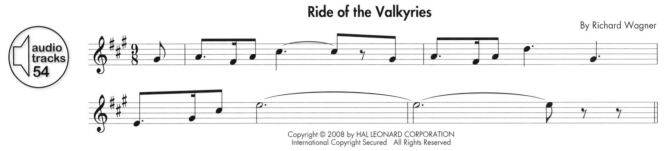

Here is a very popular request at classical trumpet auditions. This piece gives you an opportunity to practice your double-tonguing skills. *Con sordino* means "with mute." See chapter 16 for more on mutes.

Fêtes
from THREE NOCTURNES

Music by Claude Debussy

This excerpt from the symphonic poem *Also Sprach Zarathustra*, by Strauss, was inspired by the philosophical work of the same title by Friedrich Nietzsche. It is one of the most widely recognized pieces of classical music in the last 125 years and was used in the 1968 film *2001: A Space Odyssey*. There are several parts to play, so take a lower one if you can't yet play the high one.

Also Sprach Zarathustra
Opening Theme

By Richard Strauss

"The Trumpet Shall Sound" appears in Handel's oratorio *Messiah*. Handel wrote the *Messiah* in the summer of 1741 and it is one of the most popular western choral works. This brief excerpt from "The Trumpet Shall Sound" is often played on the piccolo trumpet, the instrument you hear Colin Oldberg playing on the CD.

Trumpet Shall Sound
from MESSIAH

By George Frideric Handel

Here's a brief excerpt from a beautiful piece, *Magnificat*, by Johann Sebastian Bach, written originally in 1723, but rescored to the key of D in 1733 to take advantage of trumpet resonance in that key. This was originally played on a natural trumpet (no valves) because the valve wasn't around until early in the nineteenth century. This excerpt is often played on the piccolo trumpet, the instrument you hear Colin playing on the CD.

Magnificat

By Johann Sebastian Bach

*Use 3rd valve for the upper A in the trill.

MORE DIFFICULT POPULAR MUSIC

Here are some more examples from pop music. You'll notice that these are tougher rhythmically and higher in range. It may take you some time to get your fingers and your range to this level. Keep at it! Buy the recordings and listen to the tunes so you have them in your ears while you work on your chops. Some tunes are also given in a lower octave so you can still play along if the high version is beyond reach.

An *accent* (AK-sent) is an arrow-shaped articulation drawn over or under a note. Accented notes are given more emphasis. Use more air and a stronger tongue strike to achieve this.

This tune is by the Mighty Mighty Bosstones, from the album *Let's Face It*. It's a tough tune rhythmically, and placing those accents can be tricky. Listen to the original.

The Impression That I Get

Words and Music by
Dicky Barrett and Joe Gittleman

This tune is from the album *Blood, Sweat, & Tears Greatest Hits*. Try it in the lower octave (*8vb*) if you can't reach the higher notes. Listen to the original recording.

Lucretia Mac Evil

Words and Music by
David Clayton Thomas

Lucretia Mac Evil
8vb

Earth Wind & Fire is one of the best horn bands from the seventies. This tune can be found on *Essential Earth Wind & Fire*. You have two options for this tune: high and low. In the low version, the lowest note is a pedal tone F which can be tricky. For more information about pedal tones see chapter 11.

In the Stone

Words and Music by Maurice White,
David Foster and Allee Willis

In the Stone

8vb

Lead Sheets

I always tell my students, "Music is *not* notes on a page!" Musical notation is just an approximation of the sounds you hear, no matter how precise that notation may be. If you listen to two different symphonies playing the same piece, they will express the exact same written music in different ways. If you see a standard jazz melody written out, the version you hear Miles Davis, Freddie Hubbard, or Clifford Brown play will probably be quite different from what is on the page. Music is *not* notes on a page.

The written music for "Dark Eyes" below is written in the *lead sheet* style. This means that what you see and what you hear will be slightly different. The notes you see are a simplified version of the melody you hear on the recording. If you play the notes exactly as they are on the page, you will sound fine. Once you get the fingering down, try to play along with the CD to get the other little details. For support go to www.sol-ut.com.

After the melody is played two times, the players get to *improvise*, which means one player at a time (in this case it's me on trumpet and then Sean on piano) make up whatever they want. After the improvised solos are finished, the melody comes back again and the tune ends. This is the standard way many jazz tunes are played.

Dark Eyes

Sources for Further Study

There are *thousands* of song books available to you either online or from your local music store. Even better would be for you to sit down with your favorite recordings and learn to play them by ear. Clark Terry, a jazz trumpet legend, said about the process of learning to play, "Imitate, assimilate, innovate." The *best* way to imitate is to listen and learn the music by ear. It's tough at first, but rewarding. Check out your music collection!

CHAPTER 10
TRUMPET TUNING TIPS

I don't care too much about music. What I like is sounds.

—Dizzy Gillespie (1917–1993)

What's Ahead:
- Intonation
- Basic tuning
- Pitch tendencies
- Out-of-tune notes
- Tuning with triggers
- Difference tones

Terms to Know:

tuning slide: The largest slide on the trumpet. Used to tune the entire instrument.

flat: Slightly below correct pitch.

sharp: Slightly above correct pitch.

intonation: The accuracy of pitch.

trigger: One of two slides on trumpet used to change pitch slightly; operated by the thumb and ring finger of the left hand.

concert pitch: International tuning pitch of A440. Some instruments in concert pitch are piano, flute, trombone, tuba, oboe, etc.

WHAT'S TUNING ALL ABOUT?

Sound is invisible waves of vibration. When two or more instruments create sound, the sound waves mix together. If these waves aren't synchronized so the sound vibrates at a similar wavelength, we experience this as being out of tune. The more sensitive you are to *intonation*, the more uncomfortable and even unpleasant a listening experience can be if the music is out of tune. On the other hand, if things *are* in tune, a performance can be an incredible, magical experience.

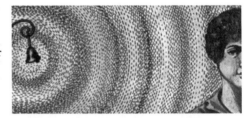

BASIC TRUMPET TUNING

The pitch of any wind instrument is a factor of length. The longer a wind instrument is, the lower its sound will be. When you tune an instrument, you're changing its pitch very slightly. This is done by either shortening or lengthening the instrument a small amount. This is done with the

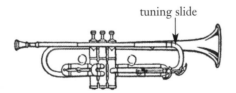

tuning slide

tuning slide. Experiment with your tuning slide: pull it almost all the way off, play a note and as you're playing, push the slide in. Do you hear it getting higher? How small of a difference are you able to hear?

Tuning the Whole Trumpet

When you move the tuning slide, you're changing the pitch of the entire horn. Trace the path of the air through the horn and you'll see that it always goes past the tuning slide before it gets redirected by the valves.

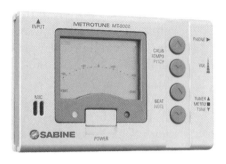

Don't guess about tuning. You *will* need a tuner. There are many different types available. Be careful not to buy a guitar tuner as they only tune six specific notes. You want a chromatic tuner that will read any pitch. Also look for an analog indication of pitch. This is a little arm that changes as your pitch changes.

Most trumpets are naturally a little bit sharp (high in pitch), so the tuning slide should be pulled out slightly whenever you play, even when you practice by yourself. This will train your ear to hear the specific pitch of your horn. All horns are slightly different, so you'll have to use the tuner to find out exactly how far out your tuning slide should be.

When you tune you want to be warmed up, relaxed, and blowing freely without any strain. This will give you a correct reading on the pitch. Play the G into the tuner.

If your tuner shows the letter name of the note you play, you'll notice that the tuner will tell you the G you played is an F. Not to worry. Trumpet notes are one letter—or a whole step—away from *concert pitch*, which is what the tuner shows. You'll learn more about this in chapter 17. Don't worry about the different letter, just watch where your pitch falls in relation to the "0" mark. Some tuners have red and green lights to indicate when you're out or in tune respectively.

Sometimes you'll adjust the pitch with your chops automatically and this will give you an incorrect reading. To avoid this, close your eyes and play the note. When you're relaxed, the air is flowing freely, and the note is steady, open your eyes and check the tuner. This will give you a more accurate reading than watching the tuner as you play the note.

If the arm is left of 0, the pitch is too low, also known as flat. Your instrument is too long so you need to shorten it to raise the pitch. Push the tuning slide in. If the arm is right of the 0, the pitch is too high, or sharp. Your instrument is too short so you need to lengthen it. Pull the tuning slide out. Close your eyes and play again. Check the pitch and continue to adjust until you're right on the 0. If you've got it, you're in tune. Well, *usually* in tune. Read on…

Things That Affect the Trumpet's Pitch

In the above tuning exercise you tuned the trumpet to the note G on the second line of the staff. This gets your horn in the right neighborhood. Other notes on the trumpet may be out of tune for several reasons. The most common reason a trumpet will go out of tune is that the horn isn't fully warmed up. Because sound waves travel faster at warmer temperatures, as the horn warms up there is a rise in frequency which is the same as a rise in pitch, also known as *going sharp*. Other reasons the pitch may change are improper breath support, very loud dynamics, very soft dynamics, high in the range, low in the range, and chop fatigue.

Play the G and watch the tuner. Your note should be in tune at first. Close your eyes and play as loudly as you can. Before you run out of air, open your eyes and check the tuner. Which way did the pitch go? Do the same exercise again, but this time keep your eyes open as you get louder and keep the little arm centered on 0. Could you do it? Keep trying until you can. Do the same exercise playing very softly. How did the pitch change?

High Pitches Tend to Be Sharp

Most players are sharp in their upper register. This can be caused by a few things, the most common being mouthpiece pressure, especially pressure on your top lip. Some players tuck their chin down and in when playing high and point the bell of the trumpet up. Sometimes we stretch the lips and use more of a "smile" embouchure when playing higher. These habits can cause the pitch to rise.

To fix these problems, keep your head level and lower you bell slightly. You may not like how this feels at first because you're not used to it. You may even lose a couple notes from your upper range. That's okay. You'll have a much better, fuller sound on the notes you *can* play and they'll be much more in tune. Hold the corners of your lips down and in. This will also fatten up your tone. Practice upper notes with the tuner. Sing them. Get help from your trumpet teacher.

Low Pitches Tend to Be Flat

Most players are flat down low, usually because not enough lip is vibrating inside the mouthpiece. The very best thing you can do is sing the notes before you play them. If you can sing the note in tune, often your body will automatically adjust to fix the pitch of the note. Amazing but true!

Use soft, slow, warm air low in your range. Pretend you're making steam come out of your mouth on a cold day. Say, "Haaaaah." Keep the volume soft to help stabilize the pitch. To raise the pitch slightly, shape your oral cavity with the "eee" vowel (raise the back of your tongue like you're saying "eee"). Practice low notes with your tuner.

The Left Hand's Role in Tuning

Another way to change the intonation of a trumpet is with the slides connected to valves one and three. Most trumpets have *triggers* on these slides which are used to move them in and out.

OUT-OF-TUNE NOTES ON TRUMPET

Even if your horn is perfectly warmed up and perfectly in tune, you still have to tune some notes. This is because there are certain notes on trumpet that are chronically out of tune. A trumpet is built so that as many notes as possible are in tune, but this leaves a few permanently out of whack. Also, certain overtones are naturally out of tune. The good news is that they're all pretty easy to fix.

The Sharp Notes

The first and worst out of tune note on trumpet is the low D♭, also known as C♯. How can two different written notes have the same pitch and the same fingering? They're called *enharmonic notes*. It's like the words *too*, *to*, and *two*: they all sound the same but have different uses.

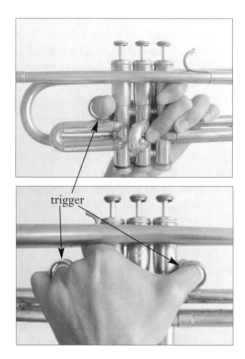

trigger

Because it's more common, I'll call this pitch C♯ from here on. If your horn is generally in tune, check the low C♯ with your tuner. You'll notice it is very sharp, or high in pitch. Before I show you the easy way to fix the pitch of this note, try to get the little arm to "0" with your chops alone. Takes some work, doesn't it?

The slide coming off the third valve is called the third-valve slide. Go figure. You'll use this slide to get that pesky C♯ in tune. Because that note is sharp, you'll need to make the trumpet longer to lower the pitch. Play the C♯ and extend the third-valve slide out until your tuner says it's in tune. The exact amount the slide should be extended depends on your horn but it's usually about an inch.

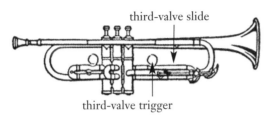

third-valve slide

third-valve trigger

Check the tuner as you push the slide out and be aware of how far out the slide is when the C♯ is in tune. That's how far you need to extend the slide **every time you play C♯**! Get in the habit of doing it every time. You *don't* need to extend the slide for *any* 123 valve combination, for example the low F♯. Use your ears to listen for your intonation, and work with that tuner.

The next worst out-of-tune note is the low D. It's also sharp, but not quite as much as the C♯. Check it with the tuner.

You'll fix the D with the same technique used to fix the C♯. Kick the third-valve slide out until the D is in tune. Make a note of where that is and *every time* you play a low D, kick the slide out that much. You can now play the worst notes on trumpet in tune every time. Make that slide kick a habit for these notes!

The next notes we'll deal with are the first line E and the second space A. Just as before, check these two notes with your tuner and try to lip them into tune. You'll see that these notes are also sharp, but only a little bit, so they won't need as much change as the previous notes. However, these notes occur a little more often, so be vigilant, especially if they're held out for a long time.

You'll also use a trigger to fix these, but this time you'll extend the first-valve slide. With your tuner, play the E and gradually extend the first-valve slide until the note is in tune. Be aware of just how far you have to move (usually less than 1/4 inch). Do the same thing with the A. The

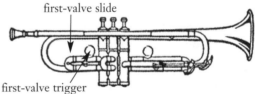

first-valve slide

first-valve trigger

distance will be about the same. If you don't have a trigger on the first valve, you'll have to tune these notes with your chops alone. Tips on that are coming soon.

The Flat Notes

The flat notes on trumpet are flat because of the way the Universe works, believe it or not. The harmonic series is a series of pitches (called *partials*) with special relationships between them. The fifth partial of the harmonic series occurs naturally a little lower than we expect to hear it. So the notes we'll be fixing are the fifth partial of the harmonic series on trumpet.

All you really need to know is that the D, E♭, and E at the top of the staff are slightly flat. By now you know the drill. Check these notes with the tuner to see how flat they are.

To fix these notes we can't use the slides because the slides only allow us to lower pitches. We need to raise the pitch of these notes. The first and best thing to do is to sing the note perfectly in tune. Find a piano or use your tuner to generate the correct pitch. Sing the note and internalize that sound. Can you hear the pitch in your head? Play and match the pitch.

You can also use the shape of your oral cavity to raise the pitch. Use the "eee" shape inside your mouth. The raised tongue will help raise the pitch. Check with your tuner to see if that's enough. If not, try playing a bit softer. Raise your eyebrows. Strange as it may seem, this actually helps. Check with the tuner.

As a last resort you can use these alternate fingerings. Use them as a last resort because the sound quality isn't nearly as good as the regular fingering. A benefit of using alternate fingerings is that you can use the triggers to change the pitch downwards if necessary.

Changing the Pitch Without a Slide

You can change the pitch of a note on trumpet with your lips alone. Try it. Play a steady G into the tuner and then make the pitch go lower (also called *pitch bending*). Did it work? How low can you make a note go before it drops down to the next note below? How slowly can you bend the note?

If you can't get the note to change at all, try lowering your jaw, loosening the muscles at the corners of your mouth, use a very deep "aaahh" to make the oral cavity as big as you can, and focus your air downward. Keep trying and get help from your teacher.

Bending the pitch upward is more challenging. Play the same G and try to make the needle of the tuner move to the right, or sharp. To help get the pitch to rise, speed up the air, shape your oral cavity using the "eeee" syllable, tighten the muscles at the corner of your mouth, and focus your air upward. Think of an upward lip slur, just before the lower note skips to the next higher note.

Bending the pitch up or down is a valuable skill to have because it allows you to fine-tune the trumpet. You can use this skill when you're playing with others and need to quickly get a note in tune. You can use it to bend the pitch of a note while playing an improvised solo. Someone adept at pitch bending can make the trumpet sound very beautiful, like a voice. Pitch bending is also helpful when you're tuning the trumpet without a tuner, and we'll cover this next. Practice pitch bending so you can bend the pitch of any note at will.

TUNING WITHOUT A TUNER

When an orchestra tunes up, the oboe player usually plays an A and the orchestra tunes to that note. In a concert or symphonic band it is often the tuba player who sets the tuning note, usually a concert B♭, and the rest of the group tunes to that note. Tuning to another instrument is much different than tuning to a tuner; it takes more awareness of pitch. Tuning to another instrument forces you to listen carefully.

Sound is vibration. To show this vibration visually, we use a wave shape. When you are out of tune, the sound waves interfere with each other. This produces "beats" in the sound. If you *are* in tune, the waves match up and the sounds blend together. If the sound is made by two like instruments (say, two trumpets), the tones will blend so much that they'll sound like one instrument.

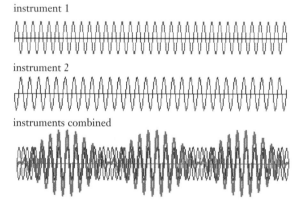

Thick, gray lines are the "beats" in the sound. Image provided by Thomas J. Henderson; *The Physics Classroom* (www.physicsclassroom.com).

FIXING POOR INTONATION BY EAR

You and a partner will each play the same note. You can also do this with a tuner that produces a tone, but doing it with another trumpet makes the beats easier to hear. Push your slide all the way in and listen for the beats. As you're playing, bend the pitch downward slowly. You'll hear the beats slow down and eventually disappear. You may bend the pitch too far downward, and in this case the beats will slow down and disappear, then start up again as you go beyond where the notes are in tune. Listen for this and try to do it.

Go the other way this time. Pull your slide out beyond the spot where the horn is in tune. Both of you play again. This time you'll bend the pitch upward to get it in tune. This is more difficult. Listen for the beats and make them disappear.

In both of the above experiments you know exactly which way to bend the pitch to get the horn in tune. In real life you may not know. This is where pitch bending comes in handy. If you can't hear which way to go to get in tune, guess. Try bending the pitch down and listen for the beats. If the beats get slower and disappear, then lower is the way to go and you need to pull your tuning slide out. If the beats speed up as you lower the pitch, then that's *not* the way to go and you should push your slide in. Continue this process until an easily blown, relaxed note is in tune.

Difference Tones

This is a great experiment to do with another trumpet player. One of you plays a C in the third space, the other plays an F on the top line. Play the notes with a full tone at a loud volume. If you're in tune you'll hear another note ring in your ear. If you're *not* in tune, all you'll hear will be a buzzing noise. One of the players must lip his or her note up or down to find where the intonation is good. When you're in tune, you'll know it because you'll hear that extra note, called a *difference tone*. To learn more about difference tones, go to http://hyperphysics.phy-astr.gsu.edu/hbase/sound/subton.html.

KEEP AT IT!

Practice these intonation skills every chance you get because it takes time to master them, but playing in tune is a valuable thing to learn as a musician. Once you learn this and can automatically play in tune, everyone who plays with you will appreciate your intonation. Like anything worthwhile, tuning takes practice for most of us. Keep listening as hard as you can, keep experimenting, and keep thinking about intonation. You can't help but get better.

CHAPTER 11

HOW LOW CAN YOU GO? PEDAL TONES

If you develop an ear for sounds that are musical it is like developing an ego. You begin to refuse sounds that are not musical and that way cut yourself off from a good deal of experience.

—John Cage (1912–1992), Composer

What's Ahead:
- What are pedal tones?
- Benefits of pedal tones
- Pedal tone exercises
- Double-pedal tones

Term to Know:

pedal tone: A pitch below the normal range of a brass instrument. Named after the foot pedals (very low notes) on the pipe organ.

PUT THE PEDAL TO THE METAL

If you've ever seen an organist in action, you've seen their feet dance around underneath the keyboard. The organist's feet are working the bass pedals of the instrument. The organ pedals are for the low notes that rattle your teeth.

Pedal tones on trumpet are notes that go below the lowest note of the trumpet, which is low F♯, seen here. If you've messed around with your horn you probably got some notes that were a lot lower than low F♯. You played a pedal tone. If you haven't experimented with very low notes, grab your horn and give it a try right now.

Don't worry too much about pitch at first; just see how low you can get. Use very loose lips and warm, slow air. Lower your jaw. Try different fingerings. If you have trouble, try using only your upper lip in the mouthpiece. To get the most benefit from pedal tones you've got to use both lips. Have your teacher or another trumpet player let you listen to some pedal tones if you're still having trouble, or listen to the CD.

WHY PRACTICE PEDAL TONES?

Pedal tones are beneficial for several reasons. They allow your embouchure to relax and they increase blood flow to the muscles used for playing. Pedal tones take a whole lot of air to produce and this will get you into good breathing habits and airflow with *all* your notes. Pedal tones are also good for ear training because the pitch of pedal tones doesn't "lock in" like normal notes on trumpet; you have to use your ears to get the pitch right.

Tone and range are also improved through the use of pedal tones, and they're an ideal warm-up technique. Pedal tones are part of my warm up every day for all of the above reasons. My chops don't feel right until I've played pedal tones for a good five minutes or more. Start practicing them now and you'll benefit from them right away.

PEDAL TONE EXERCISES

Because pedal tones are tricky to produce at first, we'll pair each pedal tone with its chord tones. Don't worry if you don't know what this means. Chord tones will help you to hear the low pedal tone you're shooting for.

Some pedal tones are easier to produce with a different fingering than you may expect. The easiest fingerings are shown first. In the exercise below you'll work down to the first pedal tone by playing the notes leading down to that low F. This will get your chops used to playing low, will help your ears hear the pitch, and will give your eyes practice reading all those ledger lines.

Do this exercise slowly. Take a HUGE breath; keep your air flowing as you descend and hold the final low note until you run out of air. Then take a HUGE breath and do it again. If at first you have trouble finding the pedal tones, get as close as you can. Use a piano to check the pitch. After a few weeks working at pedal tones, you should be able to get them fairly easily. Be persistent.

Pedal Exercise 1
Easiest fingerings are shown first with alternate fingerings next to them. Try them all.

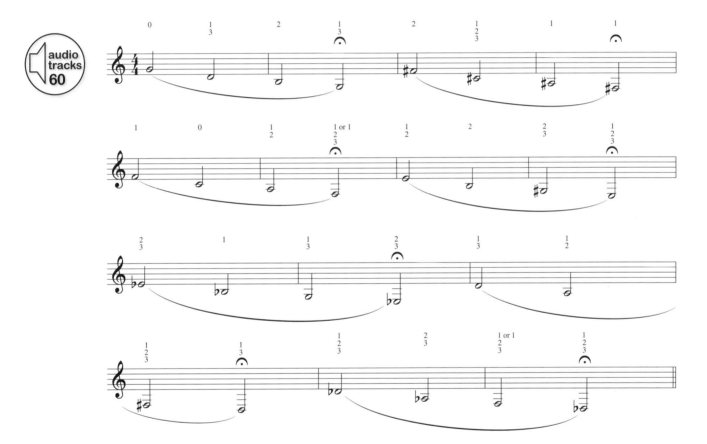

Pedal Exercise 2
This second pedal tone exercise uses the major scale to help you with pitch. When you get into the pedal tone range you must listen carefully and make the trumpet produce the right pitch. If you've been practicing your buzz, especially buzzing tunes and pitch matching, this exercise shouldn't be too much trouble. Listen! Use the piano to check your pitch. Keep at it.

Keep your air flowing all the way through these notes. Listen to the pitch. Pedal tone fingerings are marked.

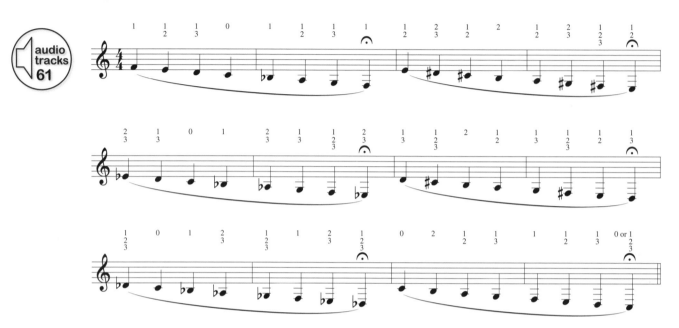

LOWER YOUR STANDARDS: DOUBLE PEDAL TONES

I first discovered pedal tones in high school. In rural Alaska, trumpet teachers were hard to find so I had to figure pedal tones out for myself. I didn't get them quite right until I got to college and was corrected. The pedal tones I had been playing were actually an octave *lower* than they should've been.

Pedal tones go lower than that pedal C you played above. In fact, these ultra-low pedal tones are often easier to play. It helps to play the note an octave or two higher to get the pitch in your ear before you play the extreme-pedal tones (also known as double-pedal tones). You might also consider using a piano to help find the pitch.

Sources for Further Study

As with any technique, you should read up and explore as many different ways to perform the technique as possible. If you'd like to hear a great tune and an example of pedal tones, listen to Nat Adderley's solo on "74 Miles Away," a tune on the album *The Best of Cannonball Adderley, The Capitol Years*. Very cool!

CHAPTER 12
HOME ON THE HIGH RANGE

The rung of a ladder was never meant to rest upon, but only to hold your foot long enough to enable you to put the other somewhat higher.

—Thomas Henry Huxley (1825–1895)

What's Ahead:

- What is high range?
- How to increase range
- Basic range exercises
- Range method books

Terms to Know:

high C: A term used by trumpet players. C two leger lines above the treble clef staff.

double high C: Also used by trumpet players. The C that is five ledger lines above the treble clef staff.

set: The specific position and flexion of an embouchure to produce a certain note. Playing high uses a different set than playing low.

WHAT IS HIGH RANGE?

High range is whatever seems high to you. For a beginner this is usually pitches above the second line G. For an average middle school player, high notes may be anything above the fourth line D. For high school players, the high notes might be above the A, first ledger line above the staff. For more accomplished trumpet players, the high range could *start* at high C. For others, the high range is up an octave beyond that, or double high C, believe it or not. Here are those notes as written.

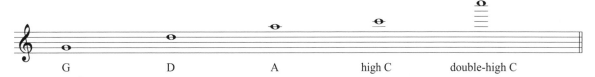

G   D   A   high C   double-high C

Don't worry about where your abilities fall in that range of ranges. Many trumpet players will never play a double high C and the majority of us won't *need* to play up that high. Probably more than 95 percent of trumpet music is below high C. The important thing is that no matter how high your range is, it can always be extended further. There is no ultimate high note on trumpet.

For great players with astounding high range, listen to Maynard Ferguson, Cat Anderson in Duke Ellington's band, Phil Driscoll, Brian Lynch, and Doc Severinsen. These are just a few jazz players. For classical music with some high trumpet parts, listen to the Brandenburg Concerto by Bach, Tchaikovsky's Fourth Symphony, or Shostakovich's Fifth Symphony. There are many more.

The other important thing is not to compare your range to someone else's range. That can be someone with either more or less range than you. Concentrate on your *own* growth as a player and find a way to let someone else's ability inspire you. Let someone else's *lack* of ability inspire you to teach them.

Don't Get Hung Up On High Range

It's important to stress that although range is a desirable goal for all trumpet players, it's not as important as musicality, good tone, flexibility, dexterity, and a few other qualities. Some trumpet players have a mentality that higher, faster, and louder is better. This is not necessarily true. *All* aspects of trumpet playing should be paid attention to, and not just range. You can have a screaming range and still be a player not many folks will want to hear. Strive for beauty.

Sometimes beauty involves the power and impact of playing high, but just sometimes. Don't get hung up on acquiring a screaming high range. Range is something that takes a lot of time to acquire, often years.

One of the biggest obstacles to increasing your range is a lack of patience. It takes time to train the muscles and hone the reflexes needed to play up high. For example, from second line G to a high C takes many players four to nine years! Building range can be done but it will take time. Expect that and embrace it and all will be well.

If you add a whole step or two to your range each six months to a year, you're doing pretty well. As you first start to practice the following exercises and make them part of your routine, you may add several notes to your upper range immediately. As you settle into the routine the progress will be less dramatic, so don't be discouraged. Just keep playing.

BEWARE OF LIP INJURY!

When playing in London, Louis Armstrong, at the end of his shows, would play 77 high Cs in a row. One night he pushed himself a little too far and severely split his lip, drenching the front of his white shirt with blood. After that he had to take a long break to let the lip heal and it was troublesome for the rest of his life. Bobby Shew tells the story of seeing blood squirt out from his mouthpiece when he played high with a lot of pressure.

It's pretty easy to damage delicate lip tissue and give yourself an injury that will take time to heal even if the injury isn't permanent. When practicing your high range, use as little pressure as you can get away with. It's better to sacrifice a note or two of range than to cram the mouthpiece into your face to get those last two notes. This is easier to say than it is to do. Use your judgment. Work with your teacher on range.

High range is affected more by your air support than lip strength. More air support will help you avoid mouthpiece pressure. Start doing sit-ups or abdominal crunches two or three times a week. In fact, regular cardiovascular exercise of some sort will help your overall playing, including your high range. Better muscle tone will improve your endurance, and stronger lungs will improve your tone, your coordination, your high range, and more.

Another excellent way to avoid injury is to rest as often as you play during practice. Resting gives your lip time to recover. In the short term, rest allows oxygenated blood to replenish the muscles in your chops. In the long term, rest allows your muscles to repair and rebuild themselves strongly.

THE LOOSE-LIP FLAP

It's appropriate that we start not with a range exercise but with a resting technique. You'll use this trick when you've been playing hard and your lips begin to feel like mincemeat. It's something you may already be doing because it's a natural reaction. This technique sounds kind of like a horse and looks pretty funny. For those reasons, if you do this when in front of an audience you may want to put your hand over your face and do it quietly.

To do the loose-lip flap, push your lips out slightly, keep them loose, and move air through them on your exhale. They should flap together and make a sound like an old Model T Ford, or a horse. Experiment with how far you need to push out your lips to get the flap started.

Yeah, it sounds funny. Can *you* do it?

The flapping massages the muscle and gets much-needed blood to your tired face. Oxygenated blood cleans out the lactic acid in muscles which causes the burn.

Can You say "Ooo-eee?"

Here is a simple technique. Without horn or mouthpiece, go back and forth between the "ooo" and "eee" shape of your lips. To increase the workout, use *isometrics*. Keep the muscles flexed throughout the movement. This pits each muscle against another and will increase the "burn."

YOUR OLD FRIEND: LIP BUZZING

Here's your old friend again. Without the mouthpiece, you *must* use the muscles necessary to produce a sound. When you buzz, strive to make the corners of your aperture move in closer. The corners of the aperture are not the corners of your lips but the edge of the buzz itself, where the lips stop vibrating.

Buzz whole notes at MM = 60. Rest four beats between each note. Go up by half steps until you can go no further, then turn around and come down by half steps. If you're using a piano to check your pitch (you should), don't skip any notes, including black keys. You might also buzz songs until your chops give out.

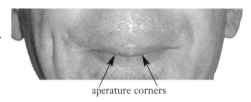

aperature corners

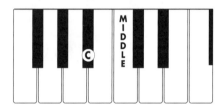

These exercises are so simple that you don't need to hear them on the CD. Just do them.

Strive for a fat, warm, steady tone. Go back down after going as high as you can. Buzz this exercise both with and without the mouthpiece. Avoid excess mouthpiece pressure.

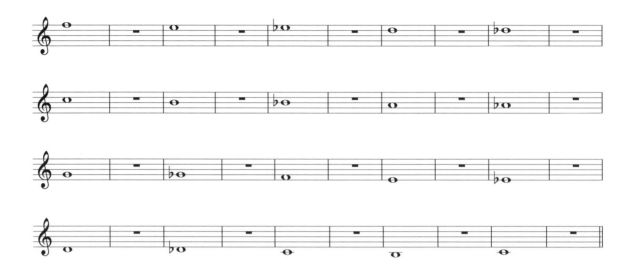

THE PENCIL EXERCISE

This exercise may seem silly, but give it a try and see if it helps you. You'll need a few pencils of different lengths so you can find one that is correct for your current chop strength. This exercise works the muscles of your embouchure responsible for producing the buzz. Pay special attention to the M. buccinators—the trumpeter's muscle—at the corners of the embouchure. These are the muscles that will do the most work during the pencil exercise.

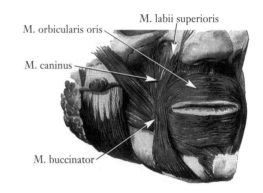

Just as with any weight lifting program, it's easy to overdo this exercise and cause damage. Take it easy at first. Don't spend a lot of time on this exercise. Do it three times a week *at the most*. Monitor how this exercise affects your sound. You may find that for the first several weeks your chops may be stiff and unresponsive and you'll have fuzzy tone. If so, spend more time practicing on the horn instead of doing this exercise.

Take the shortest pencil and put the eraser end between your lips, in front of your teeth, in the center of your mouth. Clamp your lips on the eraser and lift the pencil so it's parallel to the floor. Do this by pushing your lower lip toward your upper lip using chop muscles. *Don't thrust your jaw forward*, especially as you start to get tired. Use lip strength only. Keep your teeth slightly open and unclenched. Feel the muscles flex at the corner of your mouth.

Now take a pencil of longer length and give that a try. Move towards an unsharpened pencil once your chops are strong enough to handle it. Don't expect to hold that pencil up for very long. Players who can play the scream book all night are said to hold the unsharpened pencil up for only 4 minutes! Hold the pencil until your muscles fail. Flap your lips and stretch them out to relieve the stiffness you feel, then do it again. Here's a step-by-step breakdown.

1. Do the loose-lip flap and stretch before starting (to stretch, open your mouth as wide as you can).
2. Start with a medium- or short-length pencil. Pens also will work and are often lighter than pencils.
3. Center the pencil between the lips, in front of the teeth.

4. Hold the pencil parallel to the ground or at a slight upward angle.
5. As you begin to tire, don't thrust your jaw forward.
6. Hold the pencil in position until your lip muscles fail and the pencil drops.
7. Do the loose-lip flap and stretch your lip muscles until any stiffness or soreness fades.
8. Repeat only once or twice.
9. Go practice on the horn.

Variation

You can make the above exercise a little more intense by raising and lowering the pencil until your lip muscles fail. Don't let the pencil either drop or raise beyond a 45-degree angle, and make the movement slow and steady without thrusting your jaw forward. The slower the better (and harder) the exercise will be.

Further Study

If you're interested, here is a device that takes this pencil exercise a step or three further. Chop-Sticks™ is like a weight lifting set for your lips and it comes with a booklet containing suggestions and tips for use and a workout plan.

For more information or to get yourself a set, check out their Web site: http://www.chop-sticks.com.

LIP FAILURE STUDY

In the following exercise you'll continue to play beyond where your lip begins to fail. Toward the end of this exercise your sound will be pretty horrible. This isn't about getting a great tone (for that you should do long tones), but *is* about breaking down the muscles of your chops so they'll build up stronger.

This exercise is based on the work of the brass teacher Carmine Caruso. I've adapted it to be more accessible to beginning students. For more extensive range-building exercises, get the great book which covers these concepts and more: *Musical Calisthenics for Brass*, by Carmine Caruso.

The Foot Tap

You *must* tap your foot or use the metronome or both for this exercise. If your foot tap isn't automatic already, this exercise will be a good way to get it so. Just because the metronome is going doesn't mean you're excused from the foot tap. It's the best way to train your foot to tap in perfect time.

When you switch notes, slam down those valves precisely on the first foot tap of each note and tongue precisely on the beat.

The Embouchure

Your embouchure will be in contact with the mouthpiece the entire time and the chops will be flexed to play the entire time. *This includes rests!* Keeping the muscles flexed continuously will tire them more quickly. In addition, if you keep your embouchure set you won't have to re-form it for each new note. For beginners this makes it easier to get a note started because there is no repositioning involved.

To aid your chops as you get higher in the range, set the embouchure at the beginning of the exercise as though you were going to play the high note. With that embouchure set, relax into the first note. You may find it a little more difficult to get the lower notes out and their sound quality may suffer a little, but stay relaxed and don't be too concerned about sound quality. Setting your embouchure in this way allows you to play higher more easily later in the exercise.

The Breath
Because your embouchure is set continuously throughout this exercise, you'll need to take a full, deep breath *through your nose* only during the rests.

Lower in the range you may find you need less air. If this is the case, use the rest to exhale any excess air before inhaling again. Learn to gauge how much air you use so your lungs are emptied in the eight beats of playing. That way you can pull in a full, fresh breath during all four beats of rest.

The Airstream
The importance of the airstream can't be stressed enough. That deep breath will help provide support for high notes. This support is not so you can blow more air through your horn, but to give you the pressure you need to make the airstream very fast. Playing high actually involves *less* air moving through the horn than lower notes, but the speed of the air is much greater.

Keep the airflow fast and steady. This is important. Keep the airflow fast and steady! Think of blowing *through* the note instead of blowing the note itself. A steady, fast airstream will be heard as an unwavering, vibrant sound. This will be more difficult as your lip tires, but keep the airflow continuous throughout the exercise.

Things to Remember
1. Slur between all notes. No tonguing.
2. Avoid excessive mouthpiece pressure!
3. Keep the mouthpiece on the chops and keep the embouchure firmly set during the rests when you breathe through your nose.
4. Don't worry about sound quality as you begin to get tired.
5. Play as high as you can until absolutely no sound comes out. Don't force the notes. Do the loose-lip flap for 20 seconds, pick up where you left off and continue until no sound comes out.
6. Do the loose-lip flap. Rest for 15 minutes. You can continue with other studies during the rest period.
7. Repeat.

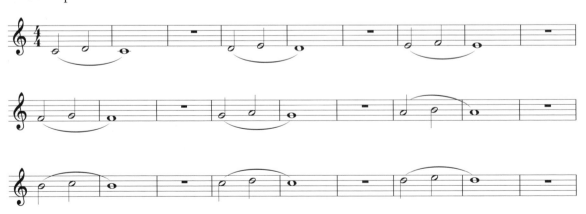

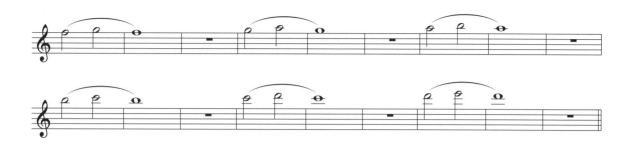

Variation

When you get bored with the key of C major, use the other 11 major keys, then the minor keys. Try a Byzantine scale when those get boring, or the Lydian augmented scale. Also, instead of playing a major 2nd between notes, try 3rds, 4ths, 5ths, etc. (If you don't know what any of this means, brush up on your music theory).

PIANISSIMO PLAYING FOR RANGE DEVELOPMENT

Playing very quietly (pianissimo) uses the same technique for playing high notes. Playing quietly with a good sound requires a fast, narrow airstream. This means your air is under compression. To focus a very tiny thread of that high pressure air you must have strong chop muscles. These are the same skills used when playing high, so a great way to improve your high range is to practice at a low or medium range as quietly as you can.

Cat Anderson was the high note specialist for Duke Ellington's band. To hear him scream, listen to Duke's band wail at the Newport Jazz Festival on the tune "Diminuendo and Crescendo in Blue." Cat Anderson said the only thing he practiced to help his range was a 20-minute G. He'd play second line G for 20 minutes at a very soft dynamic. I'm sure he stopped for air, but 20 minutes is a long time to hang on one note. I've been trying it and have noticed an improvement in range. Give it a try yourself. If nothing else, the exercise will teach you patience. Keep at it.

You Are an Air Compressor

Knowing how to compress your airstream is valuable to a trumpet player. To do it take a huge breath, close your mouth tightly, and try to push all the air out of your lungs, but don't let any air out. The pressure will build instantly, veins will begin to stand out on your neck and forehead, and you'll start to turn a lovely shade of red. Don't do it too long or you'll pass out.

To play very quietly, use this same type of pressure but let a thin, ultrafast stream of air between your chops. This will lessen the reddening and vein-popping effect a bit. Air under this high pressure is very fast and that fast airstream is crucial to playing either high or softly. In fact, without that type of fast air, a soft dynamic will be out of tune and sound weak. Experiment with how much air pressure you need.

THREE PIANISSIMO EXERCISES

The following exercises are in the key of C, but you should do them in all keys with all scales and using as many different patterns as you can create. If you're stuck and need pattern ideas, try Herbert Clarke's *Technical Studies* method book.

Pianissimo Exercise Reminders
1. Take a large breath.
2. Firm embouchure. Control the aperture. Make it small!
3. Use your chops to focus a thin stream of *fast* air.
4. Try combinations of slurring and tonguing to make these exercises more interesting and more challenging.
5. Be creative and strive always for beautiful, musical sounds!

Exercise 1
Do in all keys. Move up a half step after each repetition.

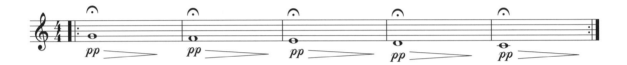

Exercise 2
Do in all keys.

Exercise 3
Do in all major and minor keys, use augmented scales, Byzantine scales, whole tone scales, pentatonics, etc., etc.

THE TWO-OCTAVE SCALE EXERCISE

Imagine you're taking a long bike ride on a cool summer day. You're about to go downhill before climbing a bigger hill. What do you do? You pedal like mad to gain speed and make the ascent of the bigger hill easier, right? This exercise is a lot like that.

It's often easier to reach the higher notes in your range if you work up to them instead of trying to nail them with no preparation. The Two-Octave Scale Exercise will help you with this. Just as with the other exercises, this one does double duty by helping you practice your scales. We'll use the G major scale as an example. Practice this technique with all diatonic scales, that is, scales that move stepwise; pentatonic scales aren't helpful because they contain large gaps between notes.

DO THIS WHILE LOOKING IN A MIRROR! A full-length mirror is best. This is an important aspect of the exercise. If you monitor yourself in the mirror, you'll catch things you're doing which you may not be aware of, like problems with your embouchure, a pivot of the horn as you go higher, poor posture, or tension in your body. Tension is a vampire which sucks out your tone quality, endurance, intonation, and range. Stay relaxed.

Each time you do this exercise, go through the following checklist. Even a slight movement or pivot of the trumpet will negate some effects of this exercise and you don't want to waste your time.

1. Stand or sit up straight and relax your entire body. Shrug your shoulders to help stay loose.
2. Form a good, balanced embouchure (say "mmmm") with firm corners and set for a medium-high note. As you play the exercise, check your lips outside the mouthpiece to be sure they are not bulging out even slightly. Embouchure should be firm all the way to the corners. Flat chin.
3. Play #1 on the next page. Take a large breath. As you descend to the low G, don't pivot the trumpet or let your embouchure relax. The tone may be poor, but keep the embouchure firm. Use warm, slow air to improve tone.
4. Repeat several times, monitor your embouchure, horn, and posture in the mirror. Be critical. Don't continue until you can do #1 in a relaxed manner and with all the correct embouchure and posture traits. Don't rush things. Take your time until you've got it.
5. Shrug your shoulders again to relax and monitor your body and face for any tension. Relax further if you find any tension.
6. Take a *large* breath, set your embouchure for the G on top of the staff, then play #2. Monitor yourself in the mirror. As before, don't pivot the horn, keep the embouchure firm.
7. As you move higher, speed up the air, focus the muscles of your embouchure towards the center as you go higher. Blow! (If you can't make it up to the G, turn around at your highest note.)
8. Repeat as many times as necessary until you can play #2 in a relaxed manner, with correct posture, embouchure, and relaxation.
9. As you gain mastery over this scale and the range, go one half step higher (A♭) and repeat the process. For more work on G, try the modes of G, or other G scales: minor, blues, Dorian, Mixolydian, Byzantine, bebop scales, etc. For a special challenge, use the chromatic scale.

Trumpet is one of the most physically demanding instruments. Take the time to be positive you're doing everything correctly. When all is correct, you'll have a powerful sensation as though your sound is shooting out of the horn like a high-pressure stream of water. Strive always for beauty of tone and expression in any range. Stick with it!

SCHEDULING YOUR RANGE WORKOUT

Don't do these exercises every day. Your muscles need time to recover and rebuild themselves. If you have no performances in the near future, take a one-day-on, two-day-off approach. This will give you three lip workouts each week and still allow enough time to let your muscles heal and rebuild.

If you have a performance coming up, lay off any range exercise at least a week before the gig. This will ensure that your chops are at their strongest when the time comes to show your stuff.

A FINAL WORD ON HIGH RANGE

The exercises in this chapter are very basic and limited and are meant to give a beginner or intermediate player some simple information to get started. Those of you who wish to progress further should check out some further materials.

Placido Domingo, the famous vocal tenor said, "The high note is not the only thing." Don't be too caught up in acquiring a high range. Work at it steadily and you will progress. Investigate all information, from books, other sources, and from real-life players. Talk to a good teacher. Good luck!

A SHORT LIST OF HIGH PLAYERS

There are a lot of players out there who can play high notes, but the list of those who can play in the stratosphere and still make beautiful music is pretty short. Here are a few of the best, all of whom are worth listening to. You can check out sound clips from most of these guys at *www.screamtrumpet.com*.

Conrad Gozzo: Sinatra, Basie, and Herman all used him because he had a fat tone, had great range, and could swing! This guy set the standard for modern lead trumpet. Check out Sinatra's *Swinging Sessions*.

Snooky Young: Long-time Basie Band player, Mr. Young also set an impressive standard for lead playing. Do you like the plunger mute? Snooky did. Listen to *Breakfast Dance and Barbecue* on the Roulette label, or anything by the Basie Band from 1950–60.

Doc Severinsen: Former long-time leader of *The Tonight Show* band, Doc is at home in any style and plays with incredible precision, artistry, and yes, range.

Bill Chase: Mr. Chase started playing lead in the Woody Herman band, and in the sixties and seventies was a pioneer of jazz rock with his own group, Chase. Listen to any Chase album.

Maynard Ferguson: The scream-trumpeter's demigod. Maynard is in many ways the epitome of the high-note specialist. Powerful, high, and exciting, MF could put on a great show, was a tireless educator, and was the inventor of the Superbone! Listen to *Message from Newport* on the Roulette label, any Stan Kenton recording from 1950–53, or any Maynard recording from 1958–64.

Arturo Sandoval: Do you like Latin music? Arturo Sandoval made great music with *Irakere* back in the seventies, and is still going strong today playing all kinds of music. A powerful and demanding musician.

Phil Driscoll: Fans of worship music will probably recognize Mr. Driscoll's name. He plays trumpet as though imitating Gabriel. Gorgeous sound and astounding range.

Jon Faddis: One of the inheritors of Dizzy Gillespie's style, Faddis is a phenomenal player with a screaming range. He currently teaches in Chicago at Columbia University.

Allen Vizzutti: Another of our modern masters of trumpet, Mr. Vizzutti has incredible chops and is at home in many different styles. If that wasn't enough, he is also a well-known composer, writer of method/etude books, and teacher at University of Washington.

Sean Jones: Mr. Jones recently accepted the position of lead trumpet with the Lincoln Center Jazz Orchestra, directed by Wynton Marsalis. He also records albums of his own work and collaborates on many other projects.

Patrick Hessions: Mr. Hessions played lead for Maynard Ferguson and has written a high-note method book, *Hessions Sessions*.

CHAPTER 13
ENDURANCE

Endurance is one of the most difficult disciplines, but it is to the one who endures that the final victory comes.

—Buddha (563–483 BCE)

What's Ahead:

- What is endurance?
- Why endurance is important
- How to gain endurance
- Resting and endurance
- Endurance exercises

Terms to Know:

perseverance: The ability to keep at something.

set: The specific set of the embouchure for a particular note.

degree: Tones in a scale. The first note of a scale is known as the first *degree* of the scale, the second as the second *degree*, etc.

HOW TO ENDURE

Endurance is one of the keys to being a good trumpet player. Endurance means being able to play through an entire concert or gig and still have chops strong enough to play what needs playing on the final piece.

The two most important things you need in the quest for greater endurance are simply patience and perseverance. It takes time to build up the efficient muscle strength you'll need to play a long gig, and the only way to get that is by working on endurance once or twice per week.

There is nothing particularly special about endurance that you need to know, but it's *essential* that your fundamentals are securely in place. If you have problems with embouchure or breathing, your endurance will suffer. Even if you're struggling with a fingering or don't have a tune entirely down, your endurance will suffer because you won't be relaxed. An important part of endurance is efficiency and it's tough to be efficient when you're tense. If you're having trouble with endurance, check with a good teacher to be sure your fundamental skills are under control.

Why Resting and Endurance Are Friends

With the following exercises, you're breaking down muscle so you can build up muscle. In order to build strength, muscles need time to rest and recuperate. *Resting is equally as important as playing.* It's easy to overdo endurance, range exercises, or playing in general. If you've experienced overplaying, you know that for a few days afterwards your chops are stiff and unresponsive. To avoid this unpleasant experience, rest early and often. A trumpet student once asked Wynton Marsalis what he does when he gets tired. He said, "I stop playing." Hey, if it works for Wynton, you should do it too. Resting helps.

When doing the exercises on the next several pages, you'll start to feel a "burn" at the corners of your mouth. This is lactic acid building up in your muscles and means you're pushing your endurance. Let the burn continue briefly, then rest and do the loose-lip flap.

Endurance Exercise Schedule

Resting is also important on a larger scale. *Don't do these exercises every day!* You'll need at least a couple days of rest to let your muscles rebuild. Doing an endurance practice session two or three times a week is plenty, and any more than that probably won't help you much and may actually hinder progress and damage chops.

Also, if you've got a gig or concert coming up, lay off the endurance practice at *least* a week before the show to ensure you'll be at your optimum chop strength for the performance. Maurice André advocates short periods of practice throughout the day to build strength and avoid injury.

The concept of resting is something we all understand but often ignore, usually because we believe *more is better* and because we want to get better and stronger as quickly as possible. Remember earlier I spoke about patience? You need it, because building endurance takes time.

The Role of Memorization

If your music is memorized, you'll free up concentration that can be used to monitor relaxation and breathing. This doesn't mean you have to do without the music. By all means, have the music in front of you as you perform. But if that music is memorized, your confidence will be greatly increased. Increased confidence means more relaxation and more ability to focus on breathing. The following exercises are simple and you should be able to memorize them in just a few sessions.

Long Tones

Remember these? Are you noticing that a lot of exercises address more than one skill? Long tones should be your best friend if you're a beginner, and an old friend if you've got some experience under you belt. You'll see a similarity between these long tones and those you did with your first notes. This is not a coincidence.

When you practice the following long tones, *breathe through your nose* just like you did in the range-building exercises in the last chapter. Keep your corners firm and embouchure set all the way through the breath. This will cause your muscles to get a continuous workout and tire more quickly. When you start to feel the burn, finish whatever note you're playing, take the horn off your face, do a loose-lip flap until the burn subsides, then continue. Limit your time on this exercise to 10–15 minutes or less, depending on your current level of endurance.

Because this book is geared toward the beginning and intermediate player, the examples below are low in the range. You can (and should) start these long tones higher in the range. Enjoy!

Endurance Exercise 1

Hold each note for one full breath and hold each rest until you're completely tanked up on air. Keep your embouchure corners set during the nose inhale. When the burn gets intense, rest with a loose-lip flap. Begin where you left off and go till you feel the burn again. For variety, do this with all scales in all patterns.

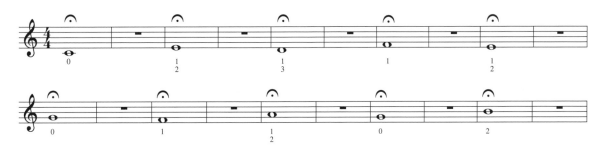

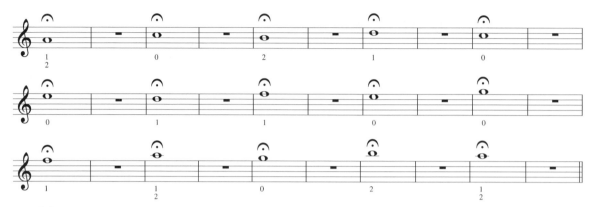

Double Duty

Did you notice the pattern in the last exercise? Because we all have limited time, it's a great idea to combine exercises to get the most benefit in the smallest amount of time. That's the reason these endurance exercises follow the patterns they do. Endurance Exercise 1 used an interval pattern of 3rds (if you don't know why it's called a 3rd, brush up on your music theory). The following endurance exercise uses the C major scale and the pattern is 1, 5, 2, 3 (these are the *degrees* of the scale and in the key of C would be C, G, D, E). Minor scales use the pattern 1, 5, 4, 3.

When practicing your endurance exercises, change the key in which you play to gain the benefit of slowly working through an unfamiliar key signature while you strengthen your endurance. Combine exercises in this way and your improvement will be that much quicker!

Endurance Exercise 2

The previous exercise had no tempo. This one does. Set your metronome to about 90 bpm (slower if you want a more intense workout), and be very strict with yourself about obeying the tempo precisely. Be sure to slam down your valves at this slow tempo to insure clean note changes. Keep your corners firm throughout this exercise, *especially* in the rests when you'll breathe through your nose.

In this exercise, when you start to feel the burn, continue for another measure before stopping to do the loose-lip flap. Once the burn goes away, continue and repeat this process.

Endurance Exercise 3

This endurance exercise involves a crescendo and a decrescendo. Start as softly as you can and crescendo to the point just before your tone starts to spread and get ugly. Hold that volume for two beats, then diminuendo back to your original soft volume. When you can't make a sound anymore, rest by doing the loose-lip flap for 20 seconds, then continue until you can't get a sound again, do the loose-lip flap for 45 seconds to a minute, and stop. Also be sure to do the variations listed after the exercise. Memorize this as soon as possible. You'll pay better attention to everything (posture, breathing, count, etc.) if you're not reading music. Music is about sounds, not notes on a page.

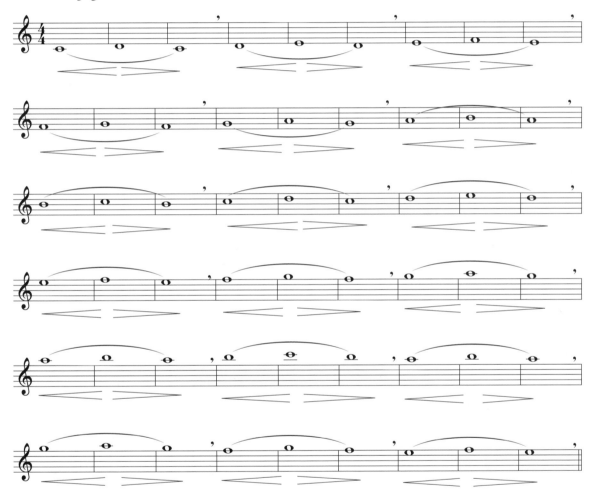

Exercise 3 Variations

Here are some variations to work through with the above endurance exercise. Practice to your weaknesses! The more double duty you can get in with your exercises the better!

- Use intervals other than the major 2nd shown above (minor 2nd or half step, major and minor 3rd, perfect and augmented 4th, perfect and diminished 5th, major and minor 6th, major and minor 7th). If you don't understand these intervals, study some music theory. Go to www.sol-ut.com for a free theory book.

- Use other scales (11 other majors, harmonic minor, melodic minor, modes, exotic scales, etc.)

- Change the dynamics: start loud, then soft, then loud.
- Go as high as you can, then go back down until you get to low C.
- Make up your own variations.

WAYS TO SAVE YOUR CHOPS

Endurance is more an exercise of efficiency than a test of strength. Techniques used to save your chops from getting tired go hand in hand with exercises used to strengthen your chops. Endurance is not simply an issue of how strong your chops are, but how you use that strength. There are a few tricks that will help save your chops so you can make it through a four-hour gig or that concert of Sousa marches.

The Breath

Remember the student who asked Wynton Marsalis a question at the beginning of this chapter? Well, the student next asked what Wynton did if stopping when tired wasn't an option. Wynton said, "I concentrate on breathing more deeply."

Because it's covered in much more detail elsewhere in the book, I'll just mention the breath here. Without good breath support, you'll tire yourself out MUCH more quickly. You should always be aware of your breath and strive to use that air to make your music. This will help save your chops more than anything else you do. As you get more and more tired, focus on your breathing! Review chapter 4.

Take It Off Your Face

A simple way to save your chops is to remove the mouthpiece from your face whenever possible, even for as short a time as an eighth rest! This technique is advocated by accomplished classical-trumpeter David Baldwin, professor at University of Minnesota. He also has other tips to help you with endurance in his article in the *International Trumpet Guild Journal* (December, 1996), "The Seven Secrets of Endurance."

THE SET OF THE EMBOUCHURE

The *set* of the embouchure means the way your chops are positioned for a particular note. For example, higher in the range the embouchure has a different set than for notes low in the range. Using the set for a low note while trying to play high will have a negative effect on range and endurance. If you're prepared for this problem, you can extend your endurance significantly.

Imagine you're about to play a phrase that has a range wider than a fourth. Before playing the phrase, note where the highest pitches are and set your embouchure for those high pitches. This may make the lower pitches sound a little less full, but the benefit is that you won't get as tired. It's much tougher to play the high pitches with the embouchure set of the low notes. Here's an exercise to help you with this idea. This exercise uses both major and minor pentatonic scales.

The major pentatonic scale uses the scale degrees 1, 2, 3, 5, and 6. Here's a theory geek brain teaser for you: The minor pentatonic scale uses the same notes as the major pentatonic scale, but in a different order. If you play the major pentatonic starting on the 6th degree (6, 1, 2, 3, 5), you'll have played the minor pentatonic.

C major pentatonic = C(1), D(2), E(3), G(5), A(6)

A minor pentatonic = A, C, D, E, G

Embouchure Set Exercise

Always look ahead so you know how high you have to play and set your embouchure accordingly.

Embouchure Set Exercise Variations

- The printed exercise is based on the C major pentatonic scale. Use all other scales.
- Add dynamics (crescendo, decrescendo) in various combinations.
- Invent another pattern instead of 1, 2, 3, 5, 6 for major and 1, 3, 4, 5, 7 for minor.

AN ENDURING MESSAGE

I can't stress enough how important it is that you rest when you practice. Your muscles need time to recover and rebuild themselves. It's also important that you rest for three or more days after doing an endurance session. This does *not* mean don't practice at all, just don't do another endurance or range session, or both, for three or more days. Your lips (and your audience) will thank you.

As with range, it takes time to develop your endurance. If you're conscientious about doing endurance exercises, you'll notice some improvement in just three or four weeks. Keep at it and in six months you'll have much more staying power and will be able to play at your peak for much longer. Keep it up!

extras

Sources for Further Study

These are just three simple endurance exercises. Of course, you should use all 12 major scales, minor scales, pentatonics, and other exotic scales with these exercises. There are many other endurance exercises out there, and you can easily make up your own to keep things interesting. Here are a couple sources to help you in your quest.

- *Musical Calisthenics for Brass*, by Carmine Caruso (Hal Leonard)
- *The Seven Secrets of Endurance*, by David Baldwin (*International Trumpet Guild Journal*, December '96)

CHAPTER 14
CLEAN UP YOUR AXE

Cleaning anything involves making something else dirty, but anything can get dirty without something else getting clean.

—Laurence J. Peter (1919–1988)

What's Ahead:
- Why clean?
- Routine cleaning
- How to take apart the trumpet
- How to fully clean the trumpet
- How to put your horn back together

Terms to Know:

axe: Slang for your instrument. Originally meant a guitar but now means any instrument.

mouthpiece brush: A brush used to clean inside the mouthpiece.

slide grease: Lubricant for the slides on the trumpet.

snake: A device used to swab out the inside of the trumpet.

valve casing brush: A brush used to clean inside the valve casings.

valve oil: Oil used on the valves to keep them moving smoothly.

lacquer: A clear sealant that keeps your horn shiny by preventing oxidation of the brass.

WHY CLEAN MY TRUMPET?

My high school biology teacher gave us an assignment: we had to run a Q-Tip over some surface and then rub that Q-Tip over mucilage in a petri dish. If any bacterium was present, it would grow quickly on the mucilage. I swabbed inside the lead pipe of my trumpet. My classmates swabbed bathroom floors, gym lockers, and other nasty places.

At the time, I cleaned my trumpet maybe once every three or four months and a good buildup of greenish slime was inside my horn. After a week my petri dish had more prolific bacterial growth than any of the others. A *lot* more. I soon began washing my horn more regularly.

Cleanliness isn't the only (or the best) reason to keep your horn clean. Your trumpet sound is produced by airflow, and the more buildup of slime you have in your horn, the less freely that air is able to flow. Also, that gunk will get into your valve casing and cause your valves to stick. Don't be like Bix Biederbecke, one of the great early jazz cornet players. He *never* cleaned his horn because he thought a clean horn sounded "hard." I can only imagine what was growing in his horn. If slime had ears, that slime in Bix's horn would've heard some great music!

Another reason to clean is that the slime in your horn actually eats away at the metal and in time will eat a hole right through it. If you keep your horn clean it will last *much* longer before repairs are necessary. There are two types of cleaning you'll do to your horn, the routine cleaning and a monthly overhaul during which you'll take apart and clean the entire horn.

ROUTINE CLEANING

If you clean certain parts of your horn every few days, you'll have less of a job when the monthly cleaning session rolls around. Here's what to do: before putting your horn away, empty the spit valves. Better yet, take the tuning slide all the way off and shake it out until it's dry. What you're emptying isn't really spit, but condensation from your breath. The damper a place is, the more likely something will grow there.

Polishing

The oil on some people's hands is corrosive enough to eat through the lacquer and even the metal of the trumpet. Others' hands have oil which is less caustic, but it still can wear through brass over time. It's a good idea to wipe your trumpet down after you play it. Music stores sell polishing cloths made specifically for instruments, but don't get an abrasive polishing cloth or use a brass polish! It will peel off your *lacquer*. Lacquer is the clear sealant that keeps your horn shiny by preventing oxidation.

I've always kept a soft cloth in my horn case to wipe away finger prints and oils from my horn. Any cloth will do, but a soft cloth is best so that you won't scratch your horn.

The Mouthpiece

The mouthpiece is an easy part of the trumpet to clean and is also a part that needs cleaning the most. It's easy. Simply swab it out with your mouthpiece brush while holding it under running water. Presto, you're done. If you're in a hurry or don't have water handy, you can use just the brush.

mouthpiece brush

Oiling the Valves

A Word of Warning: valves are the most delicate part of a trumpet and are machined to be extremely precise. Even very slight scratches, bends, or dents may ruin your valves. When handling them be very careful.

During an honor festival concert in high school my valves began to stick badly. Like the amateur I was, I had no valve oil with me on stage. I used spit instead. It worked, but not very well. Always have your valve oil handy, especially during a performance. Valves usually need oil only once every few days, depending on how much you practice.

The best and quickest way to oil a sticky valve is to take off the correct slide and drop one or two drops in each hole. The pictures show how this is done. After you've dropped the oil in, push the valve up and down a few times to distribute the oil and you're done. Two reasons this is the best way are that the valve is protected from accidental dropping, scratching, etc. and it's much faster because you don't have to unscrew the valve cap, worry about reseating the valve properly after taking it out, or screw the valve caps back on when you're done.

The very *worst* way to oil valves is to squirt oil through the holes in the caps at the bottom of the valve casings. The holes in the valve caps are there so dirt will fall *out* of them. Dirt collects in the caps and if you oil your valves through the holes you may be putting that dirt back into the valve casing. This will cause your valves to stick even more. Also, the oil has little chance to lubricate the valves and drips back out the hole, marking your pants with "trumpet tracks."

If you do take your valve out, you must seat it properly when putting it back in. Line up the number on the valve so it faces the mouthpiece. Before screwing the cap back on, twist the valve slightly until it clicks into place and won't move. This is important because if you *don't* do this, when you go to blow you'll probably give yourself a hernia. If the valve isn't aligned correctly no air will go through the horn. If this happens, twist the valve until it seats properly and try again. If you give yourself another hernia you might have the valve in the wrong slot. Check the valve number.

Greasing the Slides

Slides will rarely give you trouble between your monthly cleaning. The only time these slides will need attention is if they're sticking or are difficult to move or take off.

If one of your slides is a problem, place a little grease all the way around the farthest end of the inner part of the slide, the unlacquered part. Work just one side of the slide in and out of the horn until it's well greased. Wipe up any extra grease and then do the same with the other side of the slide. Wipe up again and put the whole slide back on the horn. You might need to wipe up extra grease one last time. Shown below are only two of your slides. If the other two are stuck, grease them the same way.

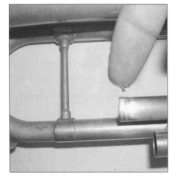

The first and third valve slides perform a vital function (tuning) and need to move quickly and smoothly. It's a good idea to add a drop of valve oil to each arm of the slide so the slide glides easily. Pull the slide almost all the way out, apply the drop, and work the slide in and out until the action is quick and smooth. If necessary, use another drop of valve oil.

TROUBLE-SHOOTING

Sometimes, especially if the horn hasn't been taken care of, slides, valve caps, and even valves will become stuck. The thing to keep in mind when working on your trumpet is that brass is a soft metal and will bend or dent easily, so be *very* careful. Don't use force. Your wisest option is to visit your local instrument repair person.

Slides

To loosen stubborn slides take a towel or piece of cloth and wrap it through the slide. Give a gentle pull and gradually increase the pressure until the slide comes out. If necessary, give some sharp tugs to loosen the slide. Hold the trumpet firmly *only* around the valve casing as you do this. If you hold the horn anywhere else, you'll probably bend it.

Valve Caps

If your valve caps are stuck, try running warm water over them. If you use pliers of some sort (this is generally a *VERY BAD* idea), wrap the horn with cloth so you don't damage it. Also, *do not* squeeze very tightly or you'll warp the valve casings and ruin your horn. If you're nervous about doing any of these things (and you should be), take your horn to a professional repairman.

Valves

If your valves are stuck, don't yank, bang, thump, thwack, or otherwise abuse them. You will very likely ruin your trumpet. The best way to loosen stuck valves is to squirt some valve oil into them through the slides. Don't unscrew the top of the valve and put valve oil there. You'll cause a mess and the oil won't get where it needs to go. If this doesn't work, let the valves soak in the tub while they're in the horn (see below for instructions), then take them out and clean them after soaking.

THE MONTHLY OVERHAUL

This process will take about an hour, but after doing it once or twice you'll be quicker. Here is what you'll need:

- A sink
- A bathtub, or something large enough to allow you to submerge your trumpet
- Clear or see-through dish soap (opaque soaps leave residue)
- An old towel and washcloth
- A cleaning rag or three
- Snake: A snake with plastic over the metal will protect your horn from scratches a little, but any snake will serve your purposes well. Don't get a trombone snake as the brushes will be a little too big for trumpet.
- Mouthpiece brush
- Valve casing brush
- Valve oil: the best oils are those that are clear and don't smell. Good brands are *Al Cass Fast, or Ultra-Pure Professional Valve Oil* (www.ultrapureoils.com).
- Slide grease: Lanolin works well, as does pretty much any commercially available grease sold at your local music store. In a pinch vaseline and a little valve oil works, too.

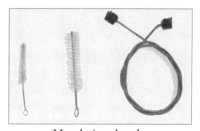

Mouthpiece brush, valve casing brush, snake

1. Spread the towel in the bottom of the tub. The towel will protect both the tub from getting scratched and your trumpet (especially the valves) from sloshing around and getting damaged. Fill the tub with soap and water to a level that will cover your trumpet. The temperature of the water should be neither hot nor cold to the touch.

> DO NOT USE HOT WATER!!! This will strip the lacquer from your trumpet and it will no longer be bright and shiny!

2. As the tub fills, place your trumpet on the counter next to the sink and pull the tuning slide. Clean it with the soap and washcloth. Run water through the slide as you clean the inside with the snake. When you're done, place the tuning slide in the tub.
3. Repeat step #2 with all the slides. As the tub fills, check the tub water level frequently!
4. Pull the first valve. Clean the holes in the valves with the valve casing brush. Be careful not to scratch the valve with the metal tip of the brush. Place the valve in the tub with the slides. Repeat with the other two valves.
5. Run the snake through the lead pipe of the trumpet, and all other pipes. Rinse with running water. Don't forget the tubes between the valves, too. Lots of gunk is hiding there. Also run the snake backwards through the horn from the bell end into the first valve casing.
6. Clean the valve casings with the valve casing brush. Don't scratch them!
7. Place the valveless, slideless trumpet into the soapy water.
8. Let the trumpet soak for 15 to 20 minutes. This will free up any crustiness there might be in the horn.
9. Drain the tub and run the snake through the slides and trumpet again as you rinse it with clean, cool water. If you're in a rush, skip the snake part, but definitely rinse the horn.
10. Dry off your trumpet and place all the parts on a counter. Be careful with the valves.

ALL TOGETHER NOW

There are a few things to remember when putting your horn back together which will help keep things clean and in the right place. It's important your horn is completely dry. Lubricants won't bond to the metal as well if the metal is wet. If you're in a hurry, a hair dryer works great, but watch out! The brass gets very hot. My horn has no lacquer. If yours does, use caution and not too much heat.

Grease with Ease

Grease is messy. Follow these tips and you'll keep the goop to a minimum. Have a rag handy because no matter how careful you are there will be some leftover grease to wipe up.

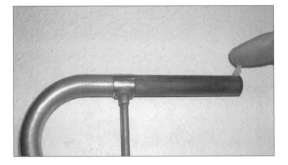

Place a little grease all the way around the farthest end of the unlacquered part of the slide. Work one side of the slide in and out of the horn until it's well greased. Wipe up extra grease and then do the same with the other side. Wipe up again and put the whole thing back on the horn. A final grease wipe up may be needed. Repeat with each slide.

Replacing the Valves

The only tricky part about putting the valves back in your horn is getting the valve in the correct place. It's funny to watch a trumpet player try to blow through a horn which has the valves in the wrong slot. Absolutely *no* air goes through the horn, the player's face turns bright red and they make a sound like *pphhhhhht!* when the air shoots out past the sides of their chops. Don't be that person.

Screw on the caps on the bottom of the valve casings. Don't tighten them too much or they'll be tough to get off. Put the valve halfway in the correct slot with the valve number facing the mouthpiece. This is important because you want to minimize any twisting of the valve in its case. Turning the valve around in the valve casing can result in horizontal scratches which will stop oil from coating the entire valve and may also cause the valve to stick. Look at the picture and notice the number stamped on the valve.

Dribble four to six drops of valve oil on the lower half of the valve, slide the valve the rest of the way in, and give it a little twist to be sure it's locked into place. Screw down the cap, then do the same thing with the other two valves.

On most trumpets each valve is stamped with its number. Valves are numbered from the mouthpiece toward the bell, so the valve closest to the mouthpiece is number one, and the valve closest to the bell is valve number three. Valve two is always easy to find. In addition to helping you put the right valve in the right slot, the number will help you position the valve correctly.

Oil the lower cylinder area of the valves (marked with a white dot) and *not* the upper part (marked with a black x).

The number *usually* faces the mouthpiece. If you put your valve in as mentioned and can't blow any air through the horn, twist the valve until it locks into place. Once the valve is locked into place, pull it out again and memorize where the number faces so you won't have to twist the valve next time you clean or remove your valves.

That's it! Keep your horn clean and happy.

Tricks and Treats

CHAPTER 15
TRUMPET SOUND EFFECTS

There is nothing more serious than fun.

—Don Cherry, trumpet master (1936–1995)

> **What's Ahead:**
> - Vibrato
> - Alternate fingerings
> - Scoops, doits, and falls
> - Half-valve technique
> - Flutter tongue and the growl
>
> **Terms to Know:**
>
> **glissando:** A smooth and continuous change from one note to another. Done on trumpet with the half-valve technique.
>
> **slide:** Another name for *glissando*. Also a name for part of the trombone.
>
> **trill:** Changing quickly from one note to another note, usually above the primary note.
>
> **scoop:** A short glissando into a note from below.
>
> **doit:** A short rising glissando after a note.
>
> **ornament:** Melodic embellishment. Ornaments may be written in or improvised by the performer. Ornaments covered in this chapter are vibrato, trills, turns, and shakes.

MAKE YOUR TRUMPET TALK!

This chapter is all about interesting and odd sounds on the trumpet. Some you might see in music for symphony, wind ensemble, or marching band; some are heard more often in jazz and other styles. The major exception to this is the vibrato, used in most styles of music.

Embellishing melodies is something that musicians have probably always done. In the baroque period, musicians were expected to add their own flourishes to melodies. The modern practice of making "novelty" sounds originated with jazz in New Orleans. Joe "King" Oliver, the mentor of Louis Armstrong, was one of the most famous early-jazz trumpet players known for making these sounds through his horn. King Oliver would often play with a handkerchief over his valves to hide what he was doing so others couldn't copy him easily.

These sounds are fun to make and folks seem to like them as long as they're not overdone. Some techniques, like the vibrato, are absolutely essential to learn no matter what style you play. A good rule with these effects is "a little goes a long way." Too much pepper in a dish ruins the taste.

THE VIBRATO

Vibrato is a type of *ornament*, something added to music to make it more beautiful. Vibrato is an ornament that is so important it gets a section all its own. Vibrato is used in all genres of music with almost all instruments. Tasteful vibrato can make a sound much more beautiful.

Vibrato is a slight raising and lowering of the pitch of a sustained note and can happen quickly or slowly. Do you notice how a violinist's left hand moves back and forth during a long note? This is vibrato. When we play a long sustained tone we vary the pitch by a tiny amount up and down to give the note more shape and beauty. An added bonus is that a good vibrato can hide any slight intonation problems.

Vibrato has two aspects: amplitude, which refers to how wide the vibrato is (think of an opera singer for an example of a wide vibrato), and frequency, which refers to how fast the vibrato is.

There are three ways to perform vibrato on trumpet: with your airstream, with your jaw, and with your hand. It's easiest to do the vibrato with your hand, so we'll cover that one first. After we cover all three techniques for vibrato, I'll tell you in more detail exactly how vibrato is used and give you exercises to get you working on your own vibrato.

The Hand Vibrato

Most of us have greater control over our hand than we do over the muscles that control breathing, and that's the reason hand vibrato is easiest. This is the vibrato technique that many players use because it's the easiest and you can achieve almost immediate results. Harry James and Rafael Méndez used this type of vibrato.

Play a second-line G and sustain it for one full breath. While the note sounds, use your right hand and *very gently* rock the trumpet forward and back about once a second. This will increase and decrease the pressure against the lips which will give you a nice oscillation of the pitch.

This should be a subtle effect, so don't use too much pressure. The motion of your hand is so slight that it's hard to see. Vary the speed at which you move the trumpet back and forth against your chops; experiment with different speeds from slow to fast.

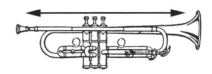

The Jaw Vibrato

Jaw vibrato is done with—you guessed it—the jaw. Hold the G as before and make a slight chewing motion with your jaw, but don't bring your teeth all the way together. You should hear a wavering of the pitch. Many players advocate the jaw vibrato because it doesn't involve added pressure on the embouchure. The jaw vibrato is perhaps the most commonly used vibrato technique in the United States.

The Airstream Vibrato

The airstream vibrato is the type that a singer or a good flute player uses. In one way this is a better type of vibrato for us trumpet players because like the jaw vibrato, it also doesn't involve adding pressure against the chops. Although it's a little harder than the hand vibrato, it's still not a very difficult technique. Try it and see which one you like better, or which one sounds better.

To get a vibrato with your air, play the second-line G and as you sustain the note, give your air a little push faster about once a second. Use the muscles of your diaphragm and stomach to give the air these pulses. Did it work for you? Keep trying until you can vary the speed of the vibrato from slow to fast.

General Vibrato Practices

There are many different styles of vibrato. A trumpet player in a mariachi band will use a much wider and faster vibrato than a symphony trumpet player (as long as the symphony player isn't playing a mariachi number), so the style of vibrato may vary depending on the type of music you're playing. As with any trumpet technique, your best course of action is to listen to accomplished players and imitate what you hear. Your best teachers are in your music collection.

That being said, there are some basic traits to vibrato you should know. Generally speaking, a long tone will start with a straight tone (no vibrato) and the vibrato will be added after a beat or two, and the waves of the vibrato will gradually speed up as the end of the note is reached. It's much better to hear this than to have it explained. Go listen to your recordings and see if you can pick out the vibrato. It's there, I guarantee it.

Only G is played here. Practice vibrato with all fingerings in all registers.

ALTERNATE FINGERINGS

One of the easiest trumpet tricks is to use an alternate fingering. Alternate fingerings are finger-ings other than the most common one. For example, the E in the fourth space is one of the most expressive notes on trumpet because it has more valve combinations than any other. The usual fingering is open. That E can also be played with third valve, first and second valve, and all three valves. A list of alternate fingerings is in the fingering chart at the back of the book.

Alternate fingerings are used to do a one-note trill or for doing some intricate rhythms on the same note. A good use of this can be heard in the second chorus of Lee Morgan's solo during the tune "The Sidewinder" on the album *The Best of Lee Morgan*, by Blue Note Records. In fact, Lee Morgan used this device a lot. Also hear Nat Adderley use it on his tune "Work Song" on the album *The Best of Cannonball Adderley, the Capitol Years*. Check it out.

Alternate fingerings can also be used to make a passage easier to finger, or to tune "problem" notes.

A good way to practice alternate fingerings is to do them in strict rhythmic patterns as well as the "flail away" approach. Below you'll see the note, its fingerings, and a sample rhythm to practice with each set of fingerings. Some fingerings are more difficult than others, and some are nearly impossible at a fast tempo.

At first, don't use your tongue at all on this exercise. Just work the valves and get the patterns as precise as you can with the fingers alone. When you've got the pattern down, try using your tongue on some of the notes. For example, tongue the first note of every measure for the whole exercise. Then tongue every beat. Then every other beat. Then try tonguing randomly. Invent variations.

Fingerings are shown as valve numbers: 0, 1, 2, 12, 23, etc. Above the rhythm for this exer-cise are the notes with their alternate fingering. If the sixteenth-note triplets in the rhythm below look intimidating to you (the second-to-the-last measure), just put six notes evenly in one beat and you'll be correct. For a variation, play the exercise backwards. Enjoy!

Don't use your tongue. Slam your valves down. Start slowly and use a metronome.

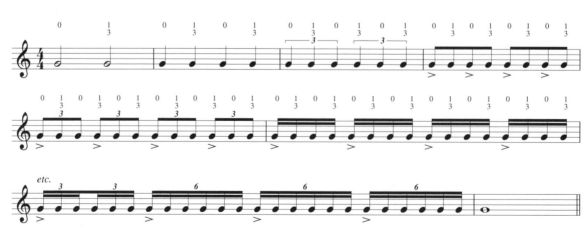

SCOOPS, DOITS, RIPS, FALLS, AND THE HORSE WHINNY

All of those strange words in the title of this section use the same technique, the *half valve*. Just like the name implies, to do it you push the valve or valves down halfway and play. It's that simple. Try it.

One of the best ways to get your trumpet talking is to use the half-valve technique. You've probably already done this accidentally when not pounding your valves down or maybe when a valve is stuck or slow coming up. Done accidentally it's not a good thing because most of the time you want note changes to be clean. The half-valve technique is great to use if you want to give your sound a more vocal quality.

One of the terms you'll see used in this section is *glissando*, which is a long smooth slide from one note to another, either upwards or downwards. *Slide* is another name for glissando. Think of a trombone playing a low note with the slide (different use of the word) fully extended. With a continuous sound, the slide is pulled in. The sound rises smoothly upwards. A downward slide on trombone sounds like a dive-bombing plane. Two other instruments that can easily produce a smooth glissando are voice and violin. On trumpet, a glissando is done with the half valve.

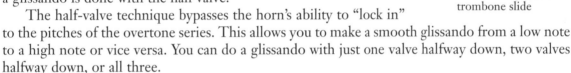

trombone slide

The half-valve technique bypasses the horn's ability to "lock in" to the pitches of the overtone series. This allows you to make a smooth glissando from a low note to a high note or vice versa. You can do a glissando with just one valve halfway down, two valves halfway down, or all three.

With all of these half-valve techniques, you've got to use a *lot* of air to make the sound stand out. Half-valve notes are much quieter than a regularly fingered note, so to make them heard you really have to blow!

Try the following. Start at a low pitch with all three valves halfway down. Make the sound go steadily upwards as far as you can, then come back down. Keep your air moving. Try it with only the first valve halfway down, then only the second valve halfway down, first and second, third and third, first and third, etc. This is the basis of all the specific techniques we'll get to next.

Just like with any special technique, a little goes a long way. Be wary of overusing this or any special technique. Overuse makes the effect less dramatic.

The Scoop

Try this. Play an F (first valve) and go to a G (open), but let your first valve come up *very* slowly. Blow steadily through the change. Did you hear that wonderful smear from the F to the G? Try it again and emphasize the smear by blowing a little harder when the valve is between notes. You can help the smear by bending the pitch with your chops as you make the change.

When you use this half-valve trick just before a note, it's called a *scoop*. Scoops are a great way to ease into a pitch and are an effective device to use while playing a melody or improvising a solo. You can do a scoop with one valve halfway down before a note, two valves halfway down, or all three halfway down. As you approach where the note falls in the rhythm, gradually let your valves come up. A scoop doesn't change the rhythm of the note at all, so you've got to start the scoop a little bit early (half of a beat or less). Starting before the note in this way doesn't alter the rhythmic placement of the scooped note. Here's what a scoop looks like written down.

In this example, the note to be scooped is on beat 4, so the scoop starts just *before* beat 4. This way once you do get to beat 4, the note is there, just as it should be.

The Doit

This is an onomonapoetic word. That means it's a word that represents a sound, like **meow**. It's pronounced *doyt* and is one syllable. A doit is also an upwards glissando, but happens after a note. Usually there is a rest after the note to give the doit some breathing space.

A doit continues upward in pitch after the note is played and can be a quick little upward sound or can last several beats as a long glissando. It's up to the performer or group leader how long the doit should be. Doits are often seen after high notes. It adds a dramatic effect when the high note is taken higher still with the doit. Here's what a doit looks like. It is from from low and high B♭.

The Rip

This is also an upwards type of glissando but is more rough sounding and does *not* use the half valve technique. Rips are a little tougher to perform because they take more air, more lip strength, and a good ear. A rip can be performed with any valve combination including open, but is easiest when done using all three valves down. During the rip, press all three valves down and blow through all the partials until you get to the target note where you quickly revert to the correct fingering for the target note.

The Fall

A fall is the opposite of the scoop and doit. A fall occurs after a note and is a downward glissando. As with the doit, there is usually a rest after the fall and the length of the glissando is up to the performer or leader. For obvious reasons, the fall usually happens after notes higher in the trumpet range.

There are two types of falls, the smooth one with the half valve, and a louder, rougher one. For the smooth fall, use the half-valve technique and *really blow* through the fall to make it heard. For the rougher fall you have a few options. One is to simply leave the valves as they are and fall off the note, also blowing hard all the way down through your range. This is difficult to do if you're not used to it. For the other option, when you fall off the note, quickly finger all three valves randomly and blow really hard. This will make the fall a little smoother than the first option and still be plenty loud. A third option is to push all three valves down as you fall off the note and again, really blow. This is like a rip in reverse. Experiment with these falls to hear the difference.

The length of the fall is decided by the performer or leader. Here's what the fall from G looks like written down. Try all four types of fall techniques described above.

The Horse Whinny

One of the fun and funnier uses of the half-valve technique is to do a horse whinny. It appears near the end of the Christmas song "Sleigh Ride." Push all three valves halfway down. You must blow hard to make the sound loud enough to be heard.

Start on a relatively low note, around second line G. Do a quick scoop up to a high G and fall off the note as soon as you start it while shaking the horn back and forth against your chops all the way down to a low pitch, around low C. Don't shake the horn too hard or you'll damage your lips. Use your ears to hear if you've got the sound right. If it sounds like a horse, you're all set. If not, try again 'til you get it.

THE GROWL AND FLUTTER TONGUING

When playing the blues, or playing with a plunger (not the one in the bathroom), growling through your horn is a great effect, especially if you're playing some "dirty" blues number. This technique is also used in some modern pieces to create a brash, in-your-face kind of sound.

The growl and flutter tongue are used sparingly and usually only for one or maybe two notes in a musical phrase. Use your judgment. Listen to other trumpet players and remember this is just a general guideline. I heard a live concert by Wynton and Branford Marsalis on NPR the other night and Wynton improvised at least a full chorus using a growl the entire time. It was a startling and masterful use of this technique. Another master of the growl and plunger combination is Cootie Williams, trumpeter for Duke Ellington. His version of "Caravan" is just about the coolest thing I've ever heard!

Though you can interchange the growl and the flutter tongue, they have a slightly different sound. Try them both and see which you prefer. Learn them both and you'll be able to choose the right sound for the right tune. You can't learn enough technique.

The Growl

The growl is the easier of these two sound effects. To do it you simply growl back in your throat as you play. Before trying it on the horn, do it without the horn. The sound you're listening for should be a rough, rumbly sound, like you're clearing your throat.

When doing a growl, we naturally use the *aahh* shape inside the mouth. This may make it tough to play a note higher in your range. While you're making the sound, practice changing the shape of the inside of your mouth with the *aahh* and *eee* vowel shapes. If you're having trouble holding a note while growling, make your oral cavity (the inside of your mouth) smaller.

Start on a second-line G or lower to try this effect, then gradually use higher and higher notes. Get yourself a plunger and use that with the growl as well. For more info on how to use a plunger, see chapter 16, *Mutes, Damfers, and Plungers, Oh My!*

Try the growl with all notes in your range. Try a melody you know well with a growl.

The Flutter Tongue

This is one case where a loose tongue is a good thing. It takes a loose tongue and steady airflow to master this technique. The tip of your tongue will hit the edge of your soft palate (that flat place just behind your teeth) very rapidly when you do the flutter tongue. Placement of the tongue is crucial; too far back and it won't work; too close to the teeth and it won't work. Looseness of the tongue is also critical. If it's not relaxed, the tongue won't move rapidly. Airflow is important to keep the tongue moving rapidly. Move that air!

If you can't get your tongue to flutter immediately, try this: with a steady airflow, touch your tongue to the middle of the roof of your mouth and gradually move it forward in your mouth toward your teeth. Think of saying "brrrrrrrrr," as if you were cold, then gradually move the tongue forward as you force the air out. Keep the tongue as loose and relaxed as you can. You should find the sweet spot where the tongue flutters easiest. If that doesn't work, try making a purring sound like a happy cat. If you can't get it, don't be discouraged; just keep trying until you can do it. Check out the CD.

Try the flutter with all notes in your range. It's especially useful in blues tunes, and with a plunger.

ORNAMENTS AREN'T JUST FOR CHRISTMAS

For a long, long time musicians have taken a given melody and added things to it to make the melody more personal, more intricate, or more interesting. *Ornaments* is the collective name of those melodic embellishments. There are a bunch of them, including trills, turns, grace notes, mordents, and lip trills (also known as shakes).

When these ornaments are written in the music you don't need to worry about when to use them. But, depending on the musical setting, all of these ornaments can be used at any time. If you're sitting third chair in a symphony orchestra, you should probably stick to what's written and not improvise your own ornamentation of the melody (if you even have the melody).

However, if you're playing lead in a jazz band, a small jazz combo, or are performing a solo, you can insert ornaments wherever you think they sound good. As with anything extra, use good taste. Listen to other trumpet players and musicians on other instruments to hear what professionals do.

Trills

Trills are a fairly common ornament in classical music, especially baroque music, and are an interesting effect. A trill is a rapid change from one note to the next higher note in the key signature, and you can see how trills are written to the left. You may see the squiggly line or just the "*tr*" in a piece of music. They mean the same thing.

The trill on an A would be played by moving rapidly between the A and the next higher note, B. Sometimes the trill is *started* on the higher note.

Trills often begin slowly, speed up to as fast as you can do the trill, then slow down again before ending on the principal tone of the trill (the written note). Below is an example of where you might find a trill in a piece of music. Two good sources for listening to trills are the second movement of the Hummel trumpet concerto and the melody of "Ceora," a tune by Lee Morgan.

Mordents

A mordent is a rapid *single* alternation between the written note and its upper neighbor (upper mordent) or its lower neighbor (lower mordent). Here's an example of each.

Turns

Another common ornament is the *turn*, which "turns" around the principal note. Turns are indicated with a symbol that looks like an "S" turned on its side. They're performed by playing the principal note (the one written), rising up to the upper neighbor tone (the note just above the principal), back to the principal, down to the lower neighbor tone (the note just below the principal), and then back to the principal note again. It's probably more difficult to read that than it is to look at the musical notation, so here you go.

Turns are a very effective ornament when used sparingly and in the right places. The final movement of the Hummel trumpet concerto has enough turns to satisfy anyone. Give it a listen and then go practice turns. Turns aren't limited to classical music, and you'll hear all the masters use this device in their treatment of a melody. Incorporate the turn into your musical tool kit.

Grace Notes

Grace notes are also known as *acciaccatura* and are easy to do. A grace note is a quick note before the principal note. Grace notes are usually performed right on the beat designated for the note, unlike the scoops above which started before the note. Grace notes are shown in written music by writing a very small note just before the principal note. Grace notes are usually only a half or whole step away from the principal note.

In a jazz setting, this type of ornament is done spontaneously.

It's probably safe to say that grace notes are more common than every other ornament except vibrato. They're a neat little effect. Practice some right now.

Appoggiatura

The appoggiatura is similar to the grace note, but longer. The term is based on the Italian word *appoggiarae* which means "to lean." The appoggiatura is more significant melodically because its length is half of the note which follows it.

The appoggiatura looks very similar to the grace note, but if you look closely, that teeny little note does *not* have a slash like the grace note does, and it is often a quarter note instead of an eighth note. Here's a written example.

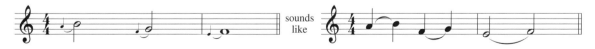

The Shake or Lip Trill

This type of ornament is simply a lip slur on steroids. The shake has been used in jazz for quite a while and can be an exciting addition when used in the right place. As with all of these other ornaments, too much use ruins the dramatic effect. Use all ornaments sparingly. Listen to your favorite players to get an idea of when to use the shake. Louis Armstrong is a master of many things, the shake included. Go listen to him.

The shake happens in the upper register of trumpet, usually above the staff. The partials are closer together in the high range and this makes shakes easiest to perform from fourth-line D on up into the range. The way to practice the shake is to first practice lip slurs lower in the range. Start on F♯ on the first space (use the 123 valve combination) and work up through all seven valve combinations. Use a metronome and gradually increase the speed until you can do four notes per beat at mm=120. You should be using the ah-ee vowel shapes inside your mouth. Something like ta-ee-ya-ee, for every beat of the metronome. Air support is crucial. Blow through the notes.

Once you can get the speed of the low notes up to four notes per click at mm=120 you're ready to take the shake above the staff. Start on the top line F♯ (123) and continue on up the valve combinations just as you did an octave lower. A slight amount of pressure in and out may help the shake up high, but be careful not to overuse mouthpiece pressure. Use your tongue and airspeed instead.

Listen to me play an excerpt from Jazzology's version of the Chucho Valdez song "Mambo Influenciado" to hear a shake used in a melody. Listen carefully and you'll also hear an upper mordent at the beginning of the excerpt.

THE BEST SOURCES FOR LEARNING COOL SOUNDS

All this information is great and should be helpful to you, but the very best way to learn cool, funny, or strange sounds on your horn is to experiment on your own. Use your creativity and imagination to think up different ways you can use that hunk of brass to make a sound nobody's heard before.

In addition to that, listen to all the trumpet players you can find, either live (definitely the best way) or on recordings. This is your very best source for discovering what trumpet sounds are out there. Listening is the best education you can give yourself on how to use those sounds tastefully. Good luck!

CHAPTER 16

MUTES, DAMPFERS, AND PLUNGERS, OH MY!

If you shoot at mimes, should you use a silencer?

—Steven Wright (1955–)

What's Ahead:

- What are mutes?
- Mute in other languages
- Basic mute use
- Types of mutes

Terms to Know:

mute: A device to alter the sound of a brass instrument. Placed in the bell of the instrument.

closed: Term used with a plunger mute to indicate the plunger covers the bell of the horn. Shown with the "+" symbol.

open: Remove mute. May be used with any mute. With the plunger mute, this is shown with the symbol "o."

back pressure: The resistance of air blown through a pipe. With a mute inserted, back pressure is greater.

WHAT IS A MUTE?

Mutes are very interesting to those who aren't musicians. Of all the questions and comments I get after a gig, the most common by far is about "those things you stick in the end of your trumpet." People like to call it a "muffler" or a "silencer" and either of those is probably a better name, because nobody has ever guessed the real term, **mute**.

A mute is something you stick into the bell of your horn to change the sound of the horn. Mutes can make your sound bright and harsh or mellow and soft, and there are even mutes that block almost all sound, a boon to a trumpet player's family members.

Here are the names of the most-used mutes: practice, straight, cup, Harmon, Wah-wah, plunger, and bucket. These types of mutes can be used effectively in many musical settings. We'll go over all of the mutes, but first check out the sidebar for a few names of mutes in foreign languages and some other basic details.

A Mute by Any Other Name

Mutes are known by different names in other languages. The Italian word for mute is *sordino*. Because most musical terms are in Italian, you'll see this one a lot. When you're supposed to put the mute in you'll see *con sordino* (with mute), and when you should take it out you'll see *senza sordino* (without mute).

In German, mutes are known as a *dämpfers*. In a piece by a German composer like Wagner, you'd see *mit dämpfer* (with mute) when the mute should be put in, and *ohne dämpfer* (without mute) when the mute is to be taken out.

Let's not leave out the French. *Avec sourdine* means "with mute," and *sans sourdine* means "without mute."

In English you'd see *with mute* and *without mute*, but you probably guessed that already. You may also see the word *open* when the mute is to be removed.

MUTES AND INTONATION

When playing with a mute one of your chief concerns is intonation. High quality mutes are usually pretty well in tune, but even the best mutes will need some tweaking to get them perfectly in tune. A mute will usually make your tone higher, but it can also make your pitch lower. If the mute makes your pitch too sharp, simply pull out the tuning slide. If the mute makes your pitch flat, you can file down the cork of the mute.

HOW TO AVOID THE ACCIDENTAL MUTE SOLO

If you've ever used a mute, you've probably had a *mute solo*, which is an accidental solo. This will happen when the entire group is quiet so that your mute solo can be heard and appreciated by all. Your mute falls out of your bell and clatters around on the floor loudly for several minutes. The embarrassment will pass, but damage to your mute might alter its intonation and harm its smooth good looks.

There are steps you can take to avoid the shame of an inadvertent mute solo and mute damage. Before you put the mute in your horn, turn the horn around and exhale a warm breath of air (haah) into the bell. This lays down a thin film of condensation which helps your mute stick inside the bell. After the breath, immediately put your mute in snugly and give it a little twist to seat it tightly.

THE PRACTICE MUTE OR THE WHISPER MUTE

This type of mute is a great help for trumpet players who must practice in an environment where making a lot of sound isn't an option. This could be a hotel room, a crowded apartment building, or even late at night in your house. With this mute the sound of the trumpet is all but silenced. You can still hear it, but it's pretty quiet.

The reason this mute is quiet is that little of the air is escaping. A practice mute has cork all the way around to seal off the air escaping from the horn and this causes a lot of *back pressure*. Blowing with a practice mute in your horn is tougher because of all that resistance.

Yamaha makes a practice mute using their Silent Brass System. It allows you to hear yourself better while playing with the mute in, includes a reverb function to enhance your sound, and allows you to pipe in a CD or MP3 player so you can play along. I just got one and love it! It is very free blowing for a practice mute, and the ability to practice anywhere, any time is invaluable. This is only one of several similar-type mutes on the market that allow you to hear yourself. Check out the others online.

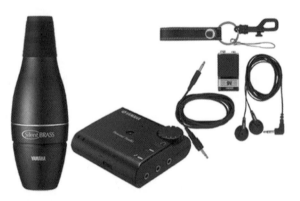

If you have the option of practicing without a mute in, by all means do it. It's much better to practice without a mute in your horn. Practice mutes are for when you have no other options but still need to get some face time in on the horn without making enemies. Occasionally a whisper mute will be called for in a piece for an ultra-soft effect.

THE STRAIGHT MUTE

The straight mute is the most frequently used mute in classical and band music. Often in these styles of music the type of mute isn't specified, you'll just see *con sordino* or something similar. If this is the case, you can bet that it's a straight mute that is being called for. If something other than a straight mute is to be used your director will tell you.

The straight mute gives the trumpet a much brighter and more piercing tone. These mutes come in a bewildering array. Some are made entirely of copper, some have copper bottoms (for a darker sound), some are stone lined, and some are plastic. They all play a little sharp and below you'll learn how to fix this.

Your best course of action is to go to your local music store and try them all out. Choose the one with the sound you like best, or the sound that you may need for a song or recording. There is no rule that says you can only have one straight mute. Buy as many as you think you need.

Cork allows the mute to stick inside your bell. Most straight mutes come with too much cork on them. You're supposed to file or sand the cork down to the proper height so the mute is in tune with your horn.

Be careful when you do this! If you file too much cork you have to buy more cork and glue it on, a time-consuming task. To avoid this, *only file a little bit at a time* and *check it with your tuner* after each filing. Most mutes have several pieces of cork around the mute. File each piece of cork equally (there are usually three pieces). Take your time and you won't botch the job and have to glue more cork back on your mute.

THE WAH-WAH, OR HARMON MUTE

The Harmon mute is one of the most interesting-sounding mutes you can stick in your horn. It's a fairly quiet mute, but if you really push some air through the horn you'll get a great sizzle from it. This is a mute Miles Davis used a lot and if you're looking for a great example, listen to Miles' version of "Autumn Leaves" and "Love for Sale" on the album *Somethin' Else*. Two classic examples of masterful Harmon-mute work.

The Harmon mute has two distinct sounds. To change the sound of the Harmon mute, mess with the stem. With the stem in, this mute is known as a wah-wah mute because of the sound you can make with it. With the stem in, the Harmon mute gets a brighter "old-timey" sound. The great thing about using the stem is that as you play, if you take your left hand and put it over the cup of the stem, then take it off, you change the quality of sound. With the stem in you can make your trumpet talk. It's a great effect and people really like it.

Jo-Ral's bubble mute produces more *buzz* than other Harmon mutes, and it looks cool.

Without the stem, the Harmon mute creates a dark, full tone that is very dramatic. Even when you're red in the face from blowing hard through this mute, it's still fairly quiet. For this reason, players often use a microphone with the Harmon mute. If you do use a microphone, you'll need to put the mute right on the mic but be careful not to hit the mic with the mute. Use your hand to feel the distance.

THE CUP MUTE

The cup mute is another popular mute and it should be obvious how it gets its name. The cup mute gives the trumpet a soft, almost hollow tone. This can make your trumpet sound more intimate, help it to blend in better with other instruments, or simply give you a quieter sound for a small dinner club.

Jo-Ral's cup mute has inserts so you can adjust the quality of the sound

You often find cup mutes used in jazz bands, swing bands, musicals, or in a small jazz combo.

Mutec's copper cup mute

THE PLUNGER

This is another fun mute and is popular with people both because of the sound it can get and because it's a tool used in the bathroom. The plunger is another great way to make your trumpet talk. Learn how to do this in detail with *Plunger Techniques*, a book by Al Grey.

A plunger made by Dennis Wick

Shown here is a commercial version of the plunger. For an equally great sound at a *much* cheaper cost, you can use an actual rubber plunger. Make sure you get the smaller sink plunger. Check your local music store or your local plumbing-supply store.

To use this mute, hold it in your left hand while you hold the horn with your right. You finally get to use the pinky-finger hook as it's meant to be used! Hold the plunger in your left hand and cover the bell with it. Does it make the pitch go higher or lower? When you use the plunger, you don't need to put it all the way over the bell. This will actually change the pitch of your note up a half step. Your aim is to change the note just a little. Play a long note and fan the plunger on and off the bell. Experiment with the types of sound you can get. Make your trumpet talk.

Another great effect often heard with the plunger is the growl or the flutter tongue. To find out how to do this fun and interesting technique, see "The Growl and Flutter Tonguing" on page 113. This is a great mute to use on blues tunes when you solo, or for the entire trumpet section in a swing band. Fun stuff!

Many players who use the sink plunger cut a hole in the top of the dome where the stick would go and place a nickel in the neck at an angle. This gives the sound more sizzle and even if it didn't get a better sound, it's a cool thing to do.

For some great recordings of plunger use, listen to Bubber Miley play the melody on "East St. Louis Toodle-oo" by Duke Ellington, or Cootie Williams, also playing with Ellington's band, on "Caravan." Another impressive use of the plunger can be heard on Wynton Marsalis's tune "The Seductress" from the album *Standard Time vol. 3*. Is that a trumpet or a voice?

Plunger mutes can be played open or closed and this is shown with a + (closed), or o (open) symbol above the note, like so:

In the last measure, move the plunger smoothly from closed to open.

THE BUCKET MUTE

The bucket mute also creates a great sound. It's got a cavernous sort of sound to it, a lot like playing into a bucket. Go figure.

Jo-Ral's bucket mute goes in the end of the bell like most other mutes, while the Hume and Berg mute clips on the end of your bell. Though the Jo-Ral is quite a bit more expensive, the ease of use and sound quality make it a good choice if you're in the market for a bucket mute.

MUTE HOLDERS

Now instead of stumbling over all those mutes you've got on the floor, you can get a mute holder to put them in. Not only will these mute holders get your mutes out from underfoot, they'll be easier to reach during a performance. Here are a few versions available to you.

Jo-Ral's mute holder

Bill Pfund's mute holder

OTHER MUTES

There are other mutes out there, like the derby mute, the Gatsby mute by Walt Johnson, the Buzz-Wow by Hume and Berg, and the Purdie mute. You can also just stick your fist in the bell to get a different sound. Invent your own mute and maybe you'll come up with a new one that will bring you wealth and fame.

CHAPTER 17

THE TRANSPOSING TRUMPETER

Be the change you wish to see in the world.

—Mahatma Ghandi (1869–1948)

What's Ahead:

- What is transposing?
- B♭ instruments
- C instruments
- The C transposition
- E♭, F, D, A♭ and E transpositions

Terms to Know:

transpose: Changing a piece of music from one key to another, keeping the relationship between pitches exactly the same.

fake book: A book of standard tunes containing only the melody and the chords. Originally used only for jazz, but there are many types of fake books now available.

C instrument: Instruments which are in concert pitch. Some are: piano, guitar, bass, flute, oboe, trombone, tuba, and bagpipes.

B♭ instrument: An instrument one whole step above concert pitch. Some are: trumpet, clarinet, treble clef baritone, and tenor sax.

TRUMPET IS A B♭ INSTRUMENT

If you've ever tried playing with a piano player or an alto sax player and used the same music, you probably noticed that things didn't sound quite right. This is because the music for these three instruments is written in different keys. Play a C on piano and it will sound like a D on trumpet or like an A on alto saxophone. Sound confusing? It is, but there's hope. You'll make sense out of it soon. Read on.

Instruments like piano, bass, guitar, trombone, flute, oboe, and violin (there are many others) are C instruments. This means that their note C is just that, a C. I know this seems weird, but stay with me.

A trumpet is what is called a B♭ instrument. Some other B♭ instruments are clarinet, bass clarinet, tenor saxophone, soprano saxophone and treble clef baritone. The lowest open note on trumpet is written as C, first leger line below the staff. The exact same *pitch* on piano is B♭. This is why trumpet is called a B♭ instrument. Here's a piano keyboard to help you with this concept.

This note on piano, a B♭, is the same pitch as

this note, a C, on trumpet

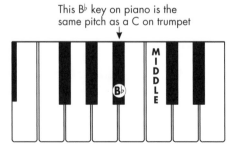

This B♭ key on piano is the same pitch as a C on trumpet

MIDDLE

You might be asking, "Wouldn't it be easier if every instrument just used the same notes as piano?" Yeah, it would be less confusing, but that's what we've been given to deal with so there's nothing to do but try to understand how it works.

If you're reading music for a C instrument, you have to adjust the notes you play on trumpet to get the right pitch. This is called *transposing*. It's a great skill to have and takes a little time to acquire, but learning to transpose is well worth the effort. If you plan on playing in a symphony, transposing to many different keys is a requirement. If you teach, you'll need to transpose in order to play duets with saxophone, French horn, and bass clef players. If you want to play jazz in a small combo using a fake book (a fake book is a book of standard tunes with only the melody and chords), you can read from a C fake book, which piano and bass players will have. If you sit down to jam with some guitar players or singer-songwriters, you'll have to transpose to get yourself into their key. All great musicians transpose the songs they're working on to *every* key.

Even if you never find yourself in any of these situations, learning to transpose is an excellent exercise for your brain and a good workout for your music-reading skills. Some transpositions are more common than others. We'll cover them in the most useful order.

THE C TRANSPOSITION

This is the most valuable and most-used transposition for trumpet players. Using this transposition will allow you to jam with guitar, keyboard, and bass players, play the trumpet parts of many symphonies, play music from a piano part, play from a C fake book, and play the part of any C instrument in treble clef (you may have to transpose piccolo and flute parts down an octave).

As I showed you on the piano keyboard before, the piano's B♭ is the same pitch as the trumpet's C. What is the interval between these two notes? How far apart are they as written? The trumpet note is written two half steps (or one whole step) *higher* than the piano note. If the concept of intervals like half steps and whole steps is new or unfamiliar to you, brush up on your music theory.

If the trumpet's written note is a whole step higher than the note for piano (a C instrument) then you now know how to transpose from one to the other. When looking at a part written for a C instrument, all the notes *you* play on trumpet need to be a whole step higher. Here's a simple and practical example of what I'm talking about. Looking at a piano keyboard will help you visualize this process.

Here is a simple melody in C, and it's transposition for B♭ trumpet. Each note of the part for B♭ trumpet is transposed *up* a whole step from version in C.

This next trumpet part is an excerpt from "Ride of the Valkyries," by Richard Wagner (also see page 70). An excellent recording of this piece is done by the Cleveland Orchestra, directed by George Szell. Check it out!

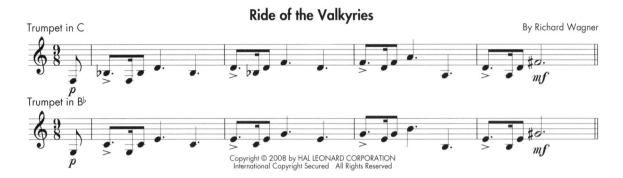

Ride of the Valkyries

Trumpet in C

By Richard Wagner

Trumpet in B♭

p =	piano. A dynamic marking that means to play softly.
mf =	mezzo forte. A dynamic marking that means to play at medium-loud volume.
> =	accent. Give this note more emphasis with tongue and air. Accents appear over or under a note.
• =	A dot after a note lengthens the note by half its original value.

Using C Transposition to Jam

When you get together with piano, guitar, and/or bass players to make sound, be aware that all those instruments are in C, so to sound like you know what you're doing, you have to transpose. This is a little simpler than transposing a written melody on the fly because you'll be dealing with keys (scales) more than individual notes. For example, if a guitar player is playing in the key of C, you'll be playing in the key of D. This means that to get the cool-sounding notes, you'll be using your D scales (major, minor, pentatonic, blues, etc.).

The tricky part about playing with string players is that they are often in sharp keys. For example, a lot of songs on guitar are in the key of E. A whole step up from E is F♯, which isn't a key that trumpet players are particularly fond of. That's only because it's unfamiliar. If you plan on playing with string players, start practicing these keys now. Here are the C transpositions for each of the keys. Notice that when you transpose keys, you're adding two sharps. The most common keys used by guitar players are in bold. Major keys are the letter on the left, and relative minor keys are on the right.

Key of Part to Be Transposed from C	Key as Transposed for B♭ Trumpet
C (no sharps or flats) Am	**D (2 sharps) Bm**
G (1 sharp) Em	**A (3 sharps) F♯m**
D (2 sharps) Bm	**E (4 sharps) C♯m**
A (3 sharps) F♯m	**B (5 sharps) G♯/A♭m**
E (4 sharps) C♯m	**F♯ (6 sharps) D♯/E♭m**
F (1 flat) Dm	G (1 sharp) Em
B♭ (2 flats) Gm	C (no sharps or flats) Am
E♭ (3 flats) Cm	F (1 flat) Dm
A♭ (4 flats) Fm	B♭ (2 flats) Gm
D♭ (5 flats) B♭m	E♭ (3 flats) Cm
G♭ (6 flats) E♭m	A♭ (4 flats) Fm
C♭ (7 flats) A♭m	D♭ (5 flats) B♭m

There is information coming up about the flats and sharps contained in each of the 12 keys. Start learning this information as soon as you can; you won't regret it. To practice these keys, start with the major scale. Learn it up and down and with as many patterns as you can.

If you want to jam with others, learn the blues scale as soon as possible. The blues scale is very common because it sounds so cool. People like it. Start with the five most-common keys, then learn the other seven. Don't neglect the minor scales in these keys either. Check out the resources at www.sol-ut.com for most of the scales you'll need. Start practicing them now!

THE OTHER TRANSPOSITIONS

Unless you're playing symphonic music, you probably won't have much use for the following transpositions. If you do plan on playing orchestral music, learning these transpositions is mandatory. We'll take care of the more common transpositions first.

Theoretically, you can transpose a part to *any* of the other 11 keys. You may be relieved to find out that there are only five or six transpositions that are commonly used. After the C transposition, the next most common are the E♭ and F transpositions. After you master those you can tackle the less frequently seen transpositions like A♭, D, E, and A.

The E♭ Transposition

Keep in mind that the trumpet is a B♭ instrument. This will help you find out how far away each transposition is from the written note. When we did the C transposition we figured that C was a whole step above B♭, and so all the notes were transposed up a whole step, right? Well, you apply that same principle to the E♭ transposition. What is the interval between B♭ (the trumpet's key) and E♭? You should come up with five half steps, or a perfect fourth. Use your keyboard to help visualize this concept.

Another way of finding a perfect fourth is to go up the major scale which begins on your starting note. Stop on the fourth note of the major scale and you have a perfect fourth. This requires you to know your major scales, which is a great idea. If you go up the B♭ major scale and stop on the fourth note what do you get? I hope you came up with E♭. Examples are always the best way to understand a concept. Here you go.

Here is the opening from the popular *Concerto for Trumpet in E♭* by Johann Hummel (also see page 67). Many players use an E♭ trumpet to play this piece, but if you transpose it, here's how. Shown are the opening phrases in E♭ and its transposition.

Trumpet Concerto in E♭ Major

Trumpet in E♭

By Johann Nepomuk Hummel

Trumpet in B♭

The E♭ transposition may take more time to get under your fingers than the C transposition did, but stick with it. As before, you could write out the transposition into E♭ (this is good practice anyway), or just learn to transpose by sight.

When learning to transpose by sight, go slowly and be aware of what key you're playing in. With an E♭ transposition, you're adding one flat to the original key signature. Here's a table with the E♭ transpositions and their respective keys transposed to B♭ trumpet keys. Major keys are on the left and the relative minor keys are on the right.

Key of Part to Be Transposed from E♭	Key as Transposed for B♭ Trumpet
C (no sharps or flats) Am	F (1 flat) Dm
F (1 flat) Dm	B♭ (2 flats) Gm
B♭ (2 flats) Gm	E♭ (3 flats) Cm
E♭ (3 flats) Cm	A♭ (4 flats) Fm
A♭ (4 flats) Fm	Db (5 flats) B♭m
D♭ (5 flats) B♭m	G♭ (6 flats) D♯/E♭m
G♭ (6 flats) E♭m	C♭ (7 flats) A♭m
G (1 sharp) Em	C (no sharps or flats) Am
D (2 sharps) Bm	G (1 sharp) Em
A (3 sharps) F♯m	D (2 sharps) Bm
E (4 sharps) C♯m	A (3 sharps) F♯m
C♯ (7 sharps) A♯/B♭m	F♯ (6 sharps) D♯/E♭m

The Order of Flats

The order of flats in a key signature is something you should memorize as soon as possible. The order of flats is BEADGCF. When written in a key signature, flats must be written on a specific line or space. A key signature with all seven flats looks like this:

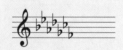

The Order of Sharps

The order of the sharps in a key signature is the order of flats backwards, or FCGDAEB. If you memorize the flat order, you've also memorized the sharp order. Here's a key signature with all seven sharps:

The F Transposition

Okay, by now you should know the drill. What is the interval between B♭ and F? To find out, go up the B♭ major scale until you get to the F. It's the fifth note, so an F transposition means you play the note a perfect fifth (seven half steps) above the written note. Remember to go slowly as you learn to read by sight in F. Whenever you transpose, it's wise to know what key you'll be playing in. For the F transposition, add one sharp to the key signature. First is the simple example, then a practical example from Debussy's Nocturne, "Fêtes" (also see page 70):

Fêtes
from THREE NOCTURNES

Music by Claude Debussy

Key of Part to Be Transposed from F	Key as Transposed for B♭ Trumpet
C (no sharps or flats) Am	G (1 sharp) Em
F (1 flat) Dm	C (no sharps or flats) Am
B♭ (2 flats) Gm	F (1 flat) Dm
E♭ (3 flats) Cm	B♭ (2 flats) Gm
A♭ (4 flats) Fm	E♭ (3 flats) Cm
D♭ (5 flats) B♭m	A♭ (4 flats) Fm
G♭ (6 flats) E♭m	D♭ (5 flats) B♭m
G (1 sharp) Em	D (2 sharps) Bm
D (2 sharps) Bm	A (3 sharps) F♯m
A (3 sharps) F♯m	E (4 sharps) C♯m
E (4 sharps) C♯m	B (5 sharps) G♯/A♭m

The D Transposition

The D transposition is a good one to know because with it you can create harmony parts on the spot. Harmony parts are often a third above or below the main melody, and this is the interval you'll use for the D transposition. More on this follows after you get the information about the transposition. As with the others, figure out the interval between B♭ and D. What did you get? It should be four half steps, or two whole steps, or a major third. Following are the examples of D transposition. The practical example is again, from "Ride of the Valkyries."

Ride of the Valkyries

By Richard Wagner

When transposing the D trumpet parts, you change keys by adding four sharps. This causes some difficulty when transposing from a key with four or more sharps because you end up with a need for double-sharps (they raise a note a whole step). Technically, you should use the double sharps, but it's easier to think in a flat key. For example, when transposing from the key of E (four sharps), you'd use the G# major scale which contains an F double sharp. Instead of using this unwieldy scale, you can think in the key of A♭, which only has 4 flats. If you've memorized your major scales and the order of sharps and flats, this will help you make these transitions more easily.

Key of Part to Be Transposed from D	Key as Transposed for B♭ Trumpet
C (no sharps or flats) Am	E (4 sharps) C#m
F (1 flat) Dm	A (3 sharps) F#m
B♭ (2 flats) Gm	D (2 sharps) Bm
E♭ (3 flats) Cm	G (1 sharp) Em
A♭ (4 flats) Fm	C (no sharps or flats) Am
D♭ (5 flats) B♭m	F (1 flat) Dm
G♭ (6 flats) E♭m	B♭ (2 flats) Gm
G (1 sharp) Em	B (5 sharps) G#/A♭m
D (2 sharps) Bm	E♭ (3 flats) Cm
A (3 sharps) F#m	D♭ (5 flats) B♭m
E (4 sharps) C#m	A♭ (4 flats) Fm

The A♭ Transposition

You won't see this one too often unless you're playing a C trumpet (a type of trumpet that plays in the key of C) and reading the music for a B♭ trumpet. Basically, it's the C transposition reversed. Instead of transposing up a whole step, you'll transpose *down* a whole step.

Use the same process to find the right interval to transpose. The A♭ is a whole step *below* the B♭, so you'd transpose down one whole step. Following are the examples:

Trumpet in A♭

Transposed for B♭ trumpet

For the A♭ transposition, add two flats to the original key signature to get the key signature you'll use for the transposition.

Key of Part to Be Transposed from A♭	Key as Transposed for B♭ Trumpet
C (no sharps or flats) Am	B♭ (2 flats) Gm
F (1 flat) Dm	E♭ (3 flats) Cm
B♭ (2 flats) Gm	A♭ (4 flats) Fm
E♭ (3 flats) Cm	D♭ (5 flats) B♭m
A♭ (4 flats) Fm	G♭ (6 flats) E♭m
D♭ (5 flats) B♭m	B (5 sharps) G♯/A♭m
G♭ (6 flats) E♭m	E (4 sharps) C♯m
G (1 sharp) Em	F (1 flat) Dm
D (2 sharps) Bm	C (no sharps or flats) Am
A (3 sharps) F♯m	G (1 sharp) Em
E (4 sharps) C♯m	D (2 sharps) Bm

The E Transposition

This is a transposition you won't see too often, but it does exist in symphony pieces, like our old favorite, Wagner's "Ride of the Valkyries." The E transposition is a little challenging because we're going up three whole steps, an interval we don't use very often. This interval is called a *tritone* because of those three whole steps. Here's a basic example of an E transposition.

Trumpet in E

Transposed for B♭ trumpet

A tritone can be explained either as a diminished fifth or an augmented fourth. Don't worry if this means nothing to you, but if it means nothing, get busy with your music theory. What it means for the key signatures is that usually you add six flats to a key signature. Where this is impractical (any key with two or more flats), you add six sharps to the key. Sound confusing? Although there is a rhyme and reason to these key signature changes, at first it's easiest if you just memorize them. If you want the rhyme and reason, study your music theory.

Still More Transposition

Yes, there are more transpositions, but by now, you should have a pretty clear idea of what's involved and you should be able to figure out for yourself how to do them. What would you do for an A transposition? Answer: go down a half step. How about a G transposition? Can you read and play from the bass clef staff? (Hint: it's very much like an E♭ transposition). Always try to push the boundary of your knowledge and ability. It's the only way to grow as a musician and as a human being.

Transposing in Foreign Languages

If you're interested in playing symphony music, you need to know how transpositions are identified in other languages. Did you ever see *The Sound of Music*? Remember the song that goes, "Do, a deer, a female deer, Re, a drop of golden sun..." Well, this little ditty is teaching you *solfege*, a system for singing written music. The notes of the solfege scale are Do (or Ut), Re, Mi, Fa, Sol, La, Ti, Do. These terms are used in many European languages to identify notes of the scale. You'll often encounter these terms when a transposition is called for.

English	French	Italian	German
B♭ piccolo trumpet	petite trompette en Si♭	Ottavino Tromba in Si♭	kleine trompete in B
F Trumpet	Trompette en Fa	Tromba in Fa	Trompete in F
E♭ Trumpet	Trompette in Mi♭	Tromba in Mi♭	Trompete in Es
D Trumpet	Trompette en Re	Tromba in Re	Trompete in D
C Trumpet	Trompette en Ut	Tromba in Do	Trompete in C
B♭ Trumpet	Trompette en Si♭	Tromba in Si♭	Trompete in B
A Trumpet	Trompette en La	Tromba in La	Trompete in A

HOW TO PRACTICE TRANSPOSITIONS

A good way to practice transposing is to get a compilation of orchestral excerpts and find pieces with the type of transpositions you want to practice. It may sound intimidating, but there are orchestral excerpts that range from simple to complex. Start with the simple ones. That way you're doing double-duty: practicing your transpositions and getting in practice on orchestral excerpts at the same time. There are several compilations of orchestral repertoire available. Talk it over with your teacher.

The main thing to remember when practicing transpositions is to take it slow and give yourself a lot of time to wrap your brain around the concept of reading a note on the page and playing a note that's different from what you see. Many people have mastered this skill, and you can, too. Remember it takes time to be able to transpose immediately at a fast tempo. Keep at it!

Sources for Further Study

Have Trumpet, Will Transpose, by Mel Broiles (Chas. Colin [somusic.com])
Duets for Two Transposing Trumpeters, by Telemann (Balquid [somusic.com])
100 Etudes, (difficult) by Ernst Sasche (International [somusic.com])
Orchestra Musician's CD-Rom Library (www.orchmusiclibrary.com)

CHAPTER 18
TRUMPET LUMINARIES

Be humble, for the worst thing in the world is of the same stuff as you. Be confident, for the stars are of the same stuff as you.

—Nicholai Velimirovic (1881–1956)

> **What's Ahead:**
> * Cornet masters
> * Orchestral masters
> * Classical solo masters
> * Jazz masters
> * Present-day luminaries

THE BEST OF THE BEST

In this chapter you may find several of the teachers you need. One of the very best ways to educate yourself is to listen, listen, listen, and then listen some more. With the exception of many of the early masters, all of these players have laid down a lot of tracks on a lot of albums. Buy them, listen to them, learn the music if you like it. Play with your favorite recordings no matter what style or what instruments are used.

The trumpet players in this chapter will be broken down stylistically. Choosing which players to include was difficult, and in order to keep this chapter shorter than it threatens to be, I've included only the most well-known or most deserving (in my opinion of course) players. My humblest apologies to you if I've left out one of your favorite players.

THE CORNET MASTERS

In the late 1800s and early 1900s, bands like John Phillip Sousa's were incredibly popular. They specialized in concert marches but played a wide variety of other light classical and original music. Remember there were no radio broadcasts until after 1920 and even at that time only relatively wealthy people had record players.

One of the primary instruments at the time was the cornet and there were many virtuosi. Here are a few in rough chronological order.

Jean Baptiste Arban (1825–1899)

Yes, this is the J.B. Arban who wrote the Arban book, the "bible" for trumpet players around the world. Nobody alive today has heard Mr. Arban, because he was born in France in 1825 and after what must have been a whole lot of practice, he had a great career as a cornet soloist. He then became a professor at the Paris Conservatory at age 32. Three years later he produced his "Cornet Method," the standard text for all brass players from cornet to tuba for the next 144 years, and it's a good bet the book will be used for a long time to come. If you don't have one, go get one.

Herbert L. Clarke (1867–1945)

Mr. Clarke was born in Massachusetts and is the author of the excellent book *Technical Studies*, which you should own. Clarke was the greatest cornet player of the early twentieth century and possibly the most famous that ever played. He got that fame from his position as the cornet soloist for John Philip Sousa's band. A few recordings exist of Clark playing solos like his composition "Shores of the Mighty Pacific" and "Bride of the Waves." Even though the earliest of these recordings dates to 1904 and are of poor quality, you'll hear a player of masterful virtuosity, technique, and artistry.

James Shepherd

Shepherd was the principal cornet player for the brass band Black Dyke and had great tone and flawless technique. It has been said that Shepherd revolutionized the art of cornet playing and serves as a bridge between the great players of the post-war period and the modern superstars of today. Listen to him play with Black Dyke on their album *High Peak*. Shepherd also recorded with his own group Versatile Brass and produced definitive versions of the classic cornet solos "Cleopatra" and "Pandora." Listen to him!

ORCHESTRAL TRUMPET MASTERS

These are the men and women few people outside the trumpet world are aware of. There are some incredible players in the orchestral tradition and there are hundreds of great recordings available of these people making music. Here are just a few orchestral trumpeters. Also check out Philip Smith (NY Philharmonic), Craig Morris (Chicago Symphony), Glen Fischthal (San Francisco Symphony), Michael Sachs (Cleveland Orchestra), Paul Beniston (London Philharmonic), and Steven Hendrickson (National Symphony).

Adolph "Bud" Herseth (1921–)

Undoubtedly the orchestral trumpet player's trumpeter. His reign at the helm of the Chicago Symphony trumpet section is legendary and long: 53 years! He retired in 2001 at age 80. Part of Mr. Herseth's success is his ability to project emotion and story in his sound. He has often demonstrated this by playing a passage with no particular concept in mind and though the notes were technically correct, the music was lifeless. He would then play the same passage again but with a story or an image or an emotion in mind and the music came alive.

If you're interested in playing orchestral music you must listen to Mr. Herseth. Get just about any recording done by the Chicago Symphony before 2001 and you'll hear him.

Roger Voisin

Roger Voisin began studying trumpet with his father, Boston Symphony Orchestra trumpeter René Voisin. Roger himself joined the Boston Symphony at the age of 17 and became principal trumpet in 1952. In 1950, he was named chair of the New England Conservatory brass and percussion department and remained at the Conservatory as its principal trumpet teacher for nearly 30 years. Mr. Voisin remains an active voice at the Boston Symphony and is on the faculty of the Tanglewood Music Center.

Mr. Voison is responsible for countless arrangements and publications of classical trumpet music. Voison retired in 1998 after *70* years of performing and teaching.

William Vacchiano

Mr. Vacchiano first began playing with the New York Philharmonic in 1935 and played for 38 years, taking the principal trumpet chair in 1942. Known for his impeccable technique, beautiful tone, and graceful legato, Vacchiano was largely responsible for the widespread modern practice of using trumpets in various keys to fit the instrument to the music more closely. He has published numerous trumpet method books and designed his own line of trumpet mouthpieces.

Just as important as his impressive orchestral contribution is Mr. Vacchiano's teaching. He began teaching professionally in 1935, taught at the Julliard School of Music for 67 years, and to this day students travel from all over the world to study with him in New York. His more well-known students include Wynton Marsalis, Gerard Schwarz, and former New York Philharmonic's principal trumpet, Philip Smith.

Susan Slaughter

Susan Slaughter joined the Saint Louis Symphony Orchestra in 1969 and four years later became the first woman ever to be named principal trumpet of a major symphony orchestra. A graduate of Indiana University, she received their coveted performer's certificate in recognition of outstanding musical performance. Ms. Slaughter has studied with Herbert Müeller, Bernard Adelstein, Arnold Jacobs, Robert Nagel, Claude Gordon, and Laurie Frink.

At the invitation of baseball commissioner Fay Vincent, Ms. Slaughter performed the National Anthem for game three of the 1991 World Series. She has served on the board of directors of the International Trumpet Guild and in 1992 Ms. Slaughter founded the International Women's Brass Conference (www.iwbc-online.org), an organization dedicated to provide opportunities and recognition for women brass musicians. In 1996, she founded Monarch Brass, an all women's brass ensemble which has toured in the U.S. and Europe.

CLASSICAL SOLOISTS

Many of the above-mentioned orchestral musicians also give performances as a soloist. Below are a few people who are well-known for their solo trumpet playing ability.

Maurice André (1933–)

When he was 30, in 1963, Mr. André began his astounding solo career. He had played trumpet in several orchestras up until this time. When he started to perform as a trumpet soloist the trumpet was not considered a solo instrument like violin or oboe. There was very little music available for a trumpet soloist. In addition, Mr. André also began using the piccolo trumpet for which there were few solo transcriptions. Today there are more than 130 transcriptions for piccolo trumpet and countless solo trumpet pieces.

Very important to André's solo career was his wife, Liliane, who became his manager and companion on his tours all over the world. In a 1978 interview he said he had done 220 concerts

Photo by Erich Auerbach/Getty Images

that year, and an average of 180 each year prior to that. That's more than 2,000 concerts! In addition to his intense touring, he has recorded over 300 albums. This man with superb technique, gorgeous tone, and wonderfully emotional playing did more for solo classical trumpet than any other person in the twentieth century.

Ludwig Güttler (1943–)

Born in the Saxony area of Germany, Ludwig Güttler is one of the more successful and impressive trumpet virtuosos of our time. Not only is he a phenomenal trumpet player (he also plays the *corno da caccia*), but he also has a great reputation as a conductor, scholar, concert promoter, and sponsor. And like most great musicians, he is also a teacher and gives master classes throughout the world.

Through his research, Güttler has brought to light a great deal of undiscovered music for trumpet, much of it from the eighteenth century. To perform these pieces he has founded the Leipzig Bach Collegium, the Ludwig Güttler Brass Ensemble, and the Virtuosi Saxoniae, which he leads as a soloist and conductor.

JAZZ TRUMPET MASTERS

Again, there are so many great players that it's tough to pick which ones to include. Players included here are not just great players, but were selected because of major contributions to music, trumpet playing, and improvement of life in general.

Photo © Michael Ochs Archives/Getty Images

Louis Armstrong (1901–1971)

Though he's best known as a trumpet player, Louis Armstrong got his start on cornet when he was allowed to play one (after much pleading) at the Colored Waif's Home in New Orleans. He had been sentenced to live in the home after a policeman caught him firing a gun in the air in celebration. He was only 12 years old. The act of giving young Louis a horn to play would shape the course of popular music to this day.

Louis was released from the Colored Waifs Home at age 14 and was befriended by Joe "King" Oliver who became Louis's idol and mentor. Armstrong began playing cornet with bands around New Orleans and at age 18 he landed a job playing with Fate Marable's band, which played on paddle wheelers that ran up and down the Mississippi. Marable's band was like going to school for Armstrong.

In addition to being the pioneer of trumpet as a solo instrument in jazz, Louis was generous and thankful to all his fans, who came to hear his music, and also came to see him off as he got on the bus. He would pass through the crowd and as he shook hands and gave his thanks, he would often press money into the hands of those who needed it and tell them to take care of themselves.

Dizzy Gillespie (1917–1993)

The first time I became aware of Dizzy was his appearance on *The Muppet Show*. Mr. Gillespie told Kermit he liked frogs, "because they can do this..." and he puffed his cheeks out alarmingly. It freaked me out and entranced me at the same time. And then he played. Wow! Now that I'm more familiar with Dizzy, I realize that that appearance was a perfect venue for his sense of humor and teaching nature.

Born John Birks Gillespie in South Carolina to a poor family, he was the ninth of nine children. He earned the nickname "Dizzy" early in his life because of his quick wit. Despite his humble beginnings, Dizzy,

Photo © Clayton Call/Redferns

with help from Charlie Parker and others, changed the shape of jazz. Dizzy was one of the originators of bebop and probably its greatest proponent and early teacher. His musical hero and early influence was trumpeter Roy Eldridge.

Though he was a monster trumpet player, Dizzy was a good pianist too. On a recording session with Charlie Parker and a young Miles Davis, Gillespie played piano and then raced over to take the trumpet part that Miles couldn't handle. Dizzy's contribution to bebop can't be overstated. He was certainly one of its greatest masters. He remains one of the most advanced trumpeters we've had yet.

Clora Bryant (1927–)

Ms. Bryant was the first woman to play with Charlie Parker, and she also played with Louis Armstrong, Dizzy Gillespie, Dexter Gordon, Carl Perkins, and Clifford Brown. She was friends with Duke Ellington. Dizzy Gillespie praised her playing. According to Scottie Barnhart, current soloist with the Basie Big Band, Clora Bryant's 1957 album *Gal With a Horn* is a must-have for any serious player of jazz, and not because the recording is made by a woman but because it's a superb combination of singing and playing. For those of you who think you have to start playing at a young age, take Ms. Bryant as an example: she started playing as a junior in high school! She made an appearance on the Ed Sullivan show and was the first female American jazz musician to play in the Soviet Union. Though she can no longer play for health reasons, Ms. Bryant still sings, lectures, and serves as a mentor for young musicians. She's a role model for trumpeters of any gender.

Miles Davis (1926–1991)

Miles has always been different, always been out on the edge looking for a new thing. This musical curiosity coupled with the fearlessness of the explorer made Miles one of the most important figures in twentieth-century music. Davis' playing continued to evolve and change throughout his life, unlike other players who found their styles and simply refined them over time. Miles' main trumpet heroes were Clark Terry, Dizzy Gillespie, and Louis Armstrong.

Photo © Express Newspapers/Getty Images

Miles played bebop with the best of them, then he took his music in a different direction with what became known as "cool jazz" in 1948. About ten years later he began playing modal jazz which has since become widely used in jazz and other genres of music. He continued to push the envelope throughout his life, experimenting with fusion and rock, and he even used electronics to shape the sound of his horn.

Photo © Metronome/Getty Images

Clifford Brown (1930–1956)

Clifford's life holds one of the most ironic tragedies of the jazz world. He started playing trumpet when he was 15 and by 18 he was playing regularly in Philadelphia. Fats Navarro, his main influence, encouraged Brown, as did Charlie Parker and Dizzy Gillespie. Brown was a virtuoso trumpet player who has influenced countless others, including Lee Morgan, Freddie Hubbard, and Woody Shaw.

Clifford only recorded for four years, and what a legacy those recordings are! In a time when some of the best players were using heroin or drinking themselves to death, Clifford Brown was a clean-living guy who didn't smoke or use drugs, and he rarely drank. All who knew him said he had a sweet disposition and gentle spirit. Though he didn't even drive a car, he died in a car accident at age 25.

Had he lived longer, Clifford Brown's influence today would be even more significant than it already is. Who knows what we missed.

Wynton Marsalis (1961–)

Wynton Marsalis has done so much to revitalize jazz that even if he wasn't an incredible player, he deserves mention here. Through an exhaustive series of performances, lectures, and music workshops, Marsalis has rekindled widespread interest in an art form that had been almost abandoned. Some of the better-known jazz musicians today have been students of Marsalis' workshops: James Carter, Christian McBride, Roy Hargrove, Harry Connick Jr., Nicholas Payton, Eric Reed, and Eric Lewis to name a few.

In 1980 at the age of 19 he earned the opportunity to join the Jazz Messengers to study under the master jazz drummer Art Blakey. In the years to follow Wynton performed with Sarah Vaughan, Dizzy Gillespie, Sweets Edison, Clark Terry, Sonny Rollins, and many other jazz legends.

In 1997 Wynton Marsalis became the first jazz musician ever to win the Pulitzer Prize for Music for his epic oratorio *Blood on the Fields*. But Mr. Marsalis's greatest legacy, in my humble opinion, is his ability to inspire not only through his own performances and compositions, but also through his character and his willingness to teach. Here is a man who

Photo by Waring Abbott/Getty Images

waited for a student in a dark, empty parking lot for an hour after a concert so the student could return home to get his trumpet for a lesson. He has been known to return calls to four-year-olds to talk to them about music. Marsalis personally funds scholarships for students attending the Tanglewood Music Center and the Eastern Music Festival. Marsalis has donated his time and talent to nonprofit organizations throughout the country.

CHAPTER 19
CHAPTER 19
HEAR HERE!

Those who do not hear the music think the dancers mad.
—African Proverb

What's Ahead:
- Why listen?
- What to listen to
- Symphonies
- Brass ensembles

Terms to Know:

brass quintet: Two trumpets, trombone, French horn, tuba.

brass quartet: Usually two trumpets, two trombones.

early music: Western-European music style before the 1600s.

baroque: Western-European music style from ~1600–1750.

classical: Western-European music style from ~1730–1825.

romantic: Western-European music style from ~1825–1900.

contemporary: Western-European classical music after 1900.

WHY LISTEN?

The reason this chapter exists is important in that listening to music requires you only to have a pair of working ears. You don't need the special skills required to actually *play* trumpet, you only need the skills required to play your radio, CD player, MP3 player, cassette player, or turntable. Or for those of you retro rebels, your 8-track, reel-to-reel machines, or Victrolas.

Recordings are the easiest and least-expensive way to experience great music made by the masters. However, it's not the *best* way to experience music. The best way is to hear music *live* being created by a warm body (or bodies) in the same room with you. There is no other experience like it and after your first good experience, you'll be hooked. After your first exposure to a live performance by a master musician, you'll be flabbergasted, astounded, amazed, and inspired. There is no substitute for live music. Listen to live musicians every chance you get.

Listening is far and away the *very* best thing you can do for your trumpet playing and your musicianship skills. There is no substitute for it. Listening to music is food for your own music. If you don't listen to other players, your road to trumpet mastery will be long and lonely. That would be sad. Consider the words of the famous philosopher Nietzsche: *Life without music would be a mistake.*

LISTEN TO WHAT?

We'll break down the broad genres of classical and jazz music into smaller parts. Included are recordings that most players believe are essential to a trumpet player's collection. My humblest apologies if I've neglected a recording you think should be mentioned. I'm always searching for more great recordings in all genres of music, so please send me the artist, title, and album name of a recording you think is important (listen@QuestionsInk.com).

We'll cover classical music (symphonies, solos, and brass ensembles), jazz (big band and combos), rock and roll, and beyond. Styles will range from the tried-and-true to the *avant garde*.

SOME LISTENING TIPS

Listening tips? Am I serious? Oh, yes, very serious. If you haven't listened to a lot of music yet, you're in for a challenge with all this unfamiliar music to listen to. If something is unfamiliar, our reaction is often one of dislike or disdain. When you first listen to a piece, try to suspend all judgment until you've listened to it several times and your ears have begun to learn it.

When I was a freshman in high school in Sitka, a small town on an island in southeast Alaska, I began to explore recorded music. At the time I wanted to find out what this whole *jazz* thing was about. I knew a few trumpeters' names and little else. I had heard of Miles Davis and figured I should get one of his albums. I chose *Bitches Brew*. Those of you who know this album are probably laughing right now. It's a highly successful jazz fusion album that was way out there to my poor untrained ears. My first reaction was, *This is jazz? I don't think I like jazz...* Fortunately, I persisted in my search and now that I have a lot more listening experience, I enjoy the album much more and I have more knowledge and appreciation of most other flavors jazz has to offer.

I hope to help you avoid any misunderstandings like I experienced back then through these lists of recordings. But even more than that, I'd like to challenge you to open up your ears and your mind to different sounds and different genres of music. Something that you may react to unfavorably on first hearing might become an old and dear friend if you keep trying to understand it. Often we dislike what we don't understand.

Then again, dislike is dislike. If you give a recording a good honest try and after several listenings it still doesn't do anything for you, forget about it and move on to something else. There is so much music in the world that you're *almost* guaranteed to find something that really moves you if you keep searching. The beautiful thing is that if you don't find what truly moves you, you can just go ahead and create it yourself!

After a couple years, come back to an album you didn't like in the past and you may be surprised to find your tastes have changed. Or not.

Okay. Let's get to the recordings.

CLASSICAL TRUMPET MUSIC

What a huge repertoire to choose from! Classical music covers a wide span of years and the earlier stuff, like Bach's music, was written before the valve, for natural trumpets. This broad genre includes arrangements of medieval music from composers like Galliard, Bird, Gibbons, and Bull, baroque composers like Bach, classical composers like Mozart, romantic composers like Beethoven, and everything up to today which also includes Stravinsky, Wagner, Tchaikovsky, and many, many more. Distilling 400 years of compositions is no easy task but I'll give it a shot.

We'll break this very large category into orchestral, small ensemble, and solo categories. In each category the music is arranged by artist and also included are title, composer, and album information. Here you go.

Orchestral Trumpet

Because much of this music has been around for a long time, there are many recordings of one piece. I'll provide you with what I (and many others) consider to be the best recordings. If you really enjoy a particular piece of music, search out other recordings. It's very interesting to hear how a piece can be interpreted by a different conductor using a different symphony.

Album Title	Composer	Conductor/Orchestra	Recording Info
Symphony No. 9 in E Minor, Op. 95	Antonín Dvorák	István Kertész/London Symphony	Penguin Classics 460604
Shostakovich	Dmitri Shostakovich	Leonard Bernstein/ New York Philharmonic	Sony: SMK 61841
Handel	George Frederic Handel	Georg Solti/ Chicago Symphony	London: D 235413
Mahler	Gustav Mahler	Klaus Tennstedt/London Philharmonic	EMI
The Planets	Sir John Holst	Eliot Gardiner/ Philharmonia Orch.	Deutsche Grammophon 445 860-2
Le Chant du Rossignol L'Histoire du Soldat	Igor Stravinsky	Pierre Boulez/ Cleveland Orchestra & Chorus	Deutsche Grammophon ASIN: B00005M9HW
Bach	Johann Sebastian Bach	Leonard Bernstein/ NY Philharmonic	Sony: SM2K 60727
Mozart	Leopold Mozart	Herbert von Karajan/ Berlin Philharmonic	EMI Classics: 7243 56696 29
Symphony 5	Gustav Mahler	George Solti/Chicago Symphony	Uni/ London Classics 30443
Mussorgsky: Pictures 1-10, Night on Bald Mountain	Mussorgsky	Guiseppe Sinopoli/ NY Philharmonic	Deutsche Grammophon 429785
Pictures at an Exhibition	Mussorgsky	George Solti/ Chicago Symphony	Uni/London Classics 30446
Pictures at an Exhibition and Other Russian Showpieces	Mussorgsky, Tchaikovsky, et al	Fritz Reiner/ Chicago Symphony	RCA 61958
1812-Festival Overture, Swan Lake, Sym. No. 6, et al	P. Tchaikovsky	George Solti/ Chicago Symphony	London/Decca Double Decker 455810
Capriccio Italien	P. Tchaikovsky	Daniel Barenboim/ Chicago Symphony	Deutsche Grammophon B000001GNO
Symphony IV	P. Tchaikovsky	George Solti/ Chicago Symphony	London/Decca Jubilee 430745
Romeo & Juliet	Prokofiev	Lorin Maazel/ Cleveland Orchestra	Decca 452970

Album Title	Composer	Conductor/Orchestra	Recording Info
Pines & Fountains of Rome	Respighi	De Waart/San Francisco Symphony	Polygram Records ASIN: B00000E2PJ
The Pines of Rome, La Mer	Respighi, Debussy	Fritz Reiner/ Chicago Symphony	Sony 68079
Strauss	Richard Strauss	Michael Tilson Thomas/ London Symphony	CBS: MK44817
Scheherazade	Rimsky-Korsakov	Hervert von Karajan/ Berlin Philharmonic	DG The Originals 463614
Scheherazade & Song of the Nightingale	Rimsky-Korsakov, Igor Stravinsky	Fritz Reiner/ Chicago Symphony	RCA 68168
Ein Heldenleben/Also Sprach Zarathustra	Strauss	Fritz Reiner/ Chicago Symphony	BMG/RCA Victor 61709
Petrouchka	Stravinsky	Zubin Mehta/ NY Philharmonic	Sony 35823
Petrouchka, Le Sacre du Printemps	Stravinsky	Pierre Boulez/ Cleveland Orchestra	Deutsche Grammophon 435769
Orchestral Excerpts	Various	Phillip Smith (frmr NY Phil. principal tpt.)	Summit Records DCD 144

Solo Classical Trumpet

Album Title	Genre	Composer	Artist	Recording Info
Trumpet Concertos	Baroque	Bach, Handel, Haydn, Vivaldi, Albinoni, Telemann, Torelli, et al	Maurice André	EMI Classics (USA) CDZB 7 69152 2
Baroque Trumpet Concertos	Baroque	Stolzel, Telemann, Vivaldi, Torelli, et al	Maurice André	Seraphim Classics CDR 72435, 7342322
The Ultimate Trumpet Collection	Various	Handel, Bach, Hummel, et al	Maurice André	Erato 92861
Trumpet Rhapsody	Classical	Artunian, Hummel, Biber, et al	Timofei Dokshizer	RCA CD 74321-32045-2
David Hickman, Trumpet	Contemporary	Kennan, Stevens, Turrin, et al	David Hickman	Crystal 668

Album Title	Genre	Composer	Artist	Recording Info
Phillip Smith, Principal Trumpet, NY Philharmonic	Various	Broughton, Turin, et al	Phillip Smith	Cala Records 513
Thomas Stevens Trumpet	Classical-Contemporary	Hindemith, Bozza, et al	Thomas Stevens	Crystal Records 761
Thomas Stevens, Trumpet	Various	Maxwell-Davies, Antheil, et al	Thomas Stevens	Crystal Records 665
Treasures for Trumpet	Various	Various	Robert Sullivan	Summit (classical) ASIN: B000066TXB
Trumpet Masterworks	Baroque-Contemporary	Inesco, et al	George Vosburgh	Four Winds ASIN: B00005UF3P
Trumpet in Our Time	Contemporary	Rouse, Korf, et al	R. Mase, M. Powell, et al	Summit (Classical) 148
American Trumpet Sonatas	Contemporary	Dello Joio, Kennan, et al	J.Harjanne, J. Lagerspetz	Finlandia 17691
Cornet Favorites	Cornet Music	HL Clarke, Simon, JB Arban, et al	Gerard Schwarz, William Bolcom, et al	Nonesuch 79157
Classic Wynton	Various	Purcell, Handel, Mouret, Bach, et al	Wynton Marsalis	Sony 60804

Brass Ensembles (2 Tpt., F. Horn, Bone, Tuba)

Album Title	Genre	Composer	Artist	Recording Info
Greatest Hits (vol. 1 & 2)	Various	Various	Canadian Brass	N/A
Bach: The Art of Fugue	Baroque	J.S. Bach	Canadian Brass	Columbia MK 44501
Plays Renaissance, Elizabethan and Baroque	Early music	Various	American Brass Quintet	Delos D/CD 3003
The Antiphonal Music of Gabrieli	Early Music	Gabrieli, Frescobaldi, et al	Cleveland Brass Ensemble, Phil. B.E.	Sony 62353
A Brass and Organ Christmas	Various	Handel, Schutz, Holst, et al	Bay Brass, Fenstermaker, et al	Gothic Records ASIN: B00004Y6PX

Album Title	Genre	Composer	Artist	Recording Info
Lollipops	Various	Mozart, Rimsky-Korsakov, et al	Phillip Jones Brass Ensemble	Claves ASIN: B00063WCM
Phillip Jones Brass Ensemble: Greatest Hits	Various	Mussorgsky, Tchaikovsky, et al	Phillip Jones Brass Ensemble	London/Decca 80702
Sousa: Stars and Stripes Forever	Marches	J.P. Sousa	Phillip Jones Brass Ensemble	London/Decca 410290
The Lighter Side	Various	Bernstein, Saint-Säens, et al	Phillip Jones Brass Ensemble	London/Decca 473185
20th Century Album	Contemporary	Copland, Britten, et al	Phillip Jones Brass Ensemble	Decca ASIN: B00060OHU

JAZZ

This style of music was born in New Orleans, experienced its heady adolescence in Chicago, New York, and Kansas City, and can now be found almost everywhere in the world. Jazz is the United States' only original art form.

As jazz is another large category, this will be broken down into solo artist/small combo and big band. In the case of the solo artist, there are so many albums to choose from that I've highlighted albums which I think are particularly enjoyable; if you don't have a lot of cash, you're likely to be quite happy with titles in bold.

Solo Jazz Trumpet

Artist	Album	Recording Info
Louis Armstrong	*Louis Armstrong: A Portrait of the Artist as a Young Man, 1923–1934*	Columbia/Legacy
	West End Blues (w/ King Oliver)	CBS
	The Hot Fives & Hot Sevens (3 albums)	Columbia
	Satch Plays Fats	Columbia
	Louis Armstrong and His All Stars Play WC Handy	Columbia
	The Louis Armstrong Story (4 albums)	**Columbia**
	The Essential Louis Armstrong (2 albums)	Vanguard
	Ambassador Satch	Columbia
	What a Wonderful World	MCA
	The Definitive Louis Armstrong	**Columbia/Legacy**
	The Majestic Years	Avid Records AVC 541
Roy Eldridge	*Little Jazz*	Inner City
	Little Jazz & the Jimmy Ryan All Stars	Fantasy

Artist	Album	Recording Info
	Roy Eldridge and His Little Jazz (3 albums)	BMG
	The Big Sound of Little Jazz	Topaz
	Art Tatum & Roy Eldridge	**Pablo**
	Happy Time	Original Jazz/Pablo
	The Nifty Cat	New World
	After You've Gone	GRP
Dizzy Gillespie	***Sonny Side Up***	**Verve**
	Diz & Getz	**Verve**
	Bird & Diz	Verve
	In the Beginning	Fantasy
	The Greatest of Dizzy Gillespie	RCA Victor
	The Champ	Savoy
	Diz & Roy	Verve
	Jambo Caribe	Verve
	Dizzy's Diamonds *(3 disc set)*	**Verve**
	Jazz at Massey Hall	Fantasy
	Concert in Paris	Roost
	Dizzy on the Riviera	PHS
Clifford Brown	*The Beginning and the End*	Columbia/Legacy
	Clifford Brown and Max Roach at Basin Street	Verve
	Study in Brown	**EmArcy/Verve**
	More Study in Brown	EmArcy
	Live at the Beehive	Columbia
	A Night at Birdland *(vol. 1 & 2)*	**Blue Note**
	Clifford Brown in Paris	Prestige
	Daahoud	Mainstream
	At Basin Street	EmArcy
	Jordu	EmArcy
	The Best of Max Roach / Clifford Brown in Concert	**GNP**
	Brown & Roach, Inc.	Blue Note
Fats Navarro	*Fats Blows*	Past Perfect
	The Fabulous Fats Navarro *(vol. 1 & 2)*	**Blue Note**
	Boppin' a Riff	BYG
	Good Bait	Roost
Miles Davis	***Kind of Blue***	**Columbia**
	Birth of the Cool	**Blue Note**
	Somethin' Else	**Blue Note**
	Miles Davis (vol. 1 & 2)	Blue Note

Artist	Album	Recording Info
	Workin'	**Prestige**
	Cookin'	**Prestige**
	'Round Midnight	Columbia
	My Funny Valentine	Columbia
	Milestones	**Columbia**
	Seven Steps to Heaven	Columbia
	Miles Smiles	Columbia
	E.S.P.	Columbia
	Cookin' at the Plugged Nickel	Columbia
	Bitches Brew	Columbia
	Live/Evil	Columbia
Lee Morgan	**Moanin' (w/ Jazz Messengers)**	**Blue Note**
	The Best of Lee Morgan: The Blue Note Years	**Blue Note**
	The Sidewinder	Blue Note
	Search for the New Land	Blue Note
	Cornbread	Blue Note
	Meet You at the Jazz Corner of the World (vol. 1 & 2)	Blue Note
	Live at the Lighthouse	Blue Note
	Lee Morgan	Blue Note
Kenny Dorham	*Horace Silver & the Jazz Messengers*	Blue Note
	The Jazz Messengers at the Cafe Bohemia (vol. 1 & 2)	**Blue Note**
	Kenny Dorham 1959	Prestige
	Whistle Stop	Blue Note
	Coltrane Time	Solid State
	Quiet Kenny	Blue Note
	Afro Cuban	**Blue Note**
Clark Terry	*Swahili*	Trip
	Oscar Peterson Trio plus 1	Mercury
	Serenade to a Bus Beat	Riverside
	Clark Terry Live at the Village Gate	**Chesky**
	Take Double	EmArcy
Freddie Hubbard	**Maiden Voyage**	**Blue Note**
	Open Sesame	**Blue Note**
	Ugetsu	Riverside
	Free for All	Blue Note
	Caravan	Riverside
	Empyrean Isles	Blue Note
	Speak No Evil	Blue Note

Artist	Album	Recording Info
	Black Angel	Atlantic
	Keystone Bop	Fantasy
	Red Clay	Sony
	Ready for Freddie	Blue Note
	The All Seeing Eye	Blue Note
	Hub Tones	Blue Note
Chet Baker	*The Most Important Jazz Album of 1964/65*	Colpix
	Mulligan Meets Konitz	**World Pacific Jazz**
	Smokin' With the Chet Baker Quintet	Roulette
	The Touch of Your Lips	Steeplechase
	Chet	Riverside
Maynard Ferguson	*This Is Jazz*	Sony
	Chameleon	Sony
	Conquistador	Sony
	These Cats Can Swing	Concord Records
	Master of the Stratosphere	Sony Special Product
	Verve Jazz Masters '52: Maynard Ferguson	Polygram Records
Woody Shaw	***Cape Verdean Blues***	**Blue Note**
	If You're Not Part of the Solution, You're Part of the Problem	Milestone
	Love Dance	Muse
	Little Red's Fantasy	Muse
	Rosewood	Columbia
	The Homecoming	Columbia
Blue Mitchell	*Blowin' the Blues Away*	Blue Note
	Silvers Serenade	Blue Note
	Horace-Scope	Blue Note
	Heads Up	Blue Note
	Boss Horn	**Blue Note**
Tom Harrell	*Silver and Brass*	Blue Note
	Silver and Voices	Blue Note
	Silver and Wood	Blue Note
	The Art of Rhythm	RCA
Art Farmer	***Modern Art***	**United Artists**
	Art	Argo
	Silk Road	Arabesque Recordings

Artist	Album	Recording Info
Doc Cheatham	*Doc Cheatham & Nicholas Payton*	**Verve**
	The Fabulous Doc Cheatham	Parkwood
	Butch Thompson & Doc Cheatham	Daring
	At the Bern Jazz Festival	Sackville
Nicholas Payton	*Payton's Place*	Verve
	From This Moment On	Verve
	Dear Louis	Verve
	Gumbo Nouveau	Verve
	Nick at Night	Verve
Wynton Marsalis	*Think of One*	**Columbia**
	Black Codes from the Underground	Columbia
	Wynton Marsalis	Columbia
	Hot House Flowers	Columbia
	The Majesty of the Blues	Columbia
	Marsalis Standard Time, vol. 1	Columbia
	Blood on the Fields	**Sony**
	Joe Cool's Blues	**Sony**
Roy Hargrove	*Parker's Mood*	**Verve**
	With the Tenors of Our Time	Verve
	Approaching Standards	Novus

More Jazz Trumpet Players

The previous list, believe it or not, is only a start. Here are some other artists you should check out: Valaida Snow, **Clora Bryant**, **Terrel Stafford**, **Nat Adderley**, **Bix Beiderbecke**, Arturo Sandoval, Terence Blanchard, **Lester Bowie**, Fabrizzio Bosso, Randy Brecker, Donald Byrd, Bill Chase, **Don Cherry**, Johnny Coles, Conte Candoli, **Dave Douglas**, Jon Faddis, Greg Gisbert, Tim Hagans, Wilbur Harden, Eddie Henderson, Ingrid Jensen, Thad Jones, Booker Little, Brian Lynch, John McNeil, Claudio Roditi, Red Rodney, **Wallace Roney**, Doc Severinson, Jack Sheldon, Bobby Shew, Ira Sullivan, Buddy Childers, Al Porcino, **Snooky Young**, Dave Stahl, Bernie Glow, Conrad Gozzo, Johnny Frosk, George Graham, Lew Soloff, Jimmy Maxwell, Laurie Frink, Peter Olstad, Roger Ingram, Dave Trigg, and **Cootie Williams**. There are more...

Big Bands with Great Trumpet Sections

Album Title	Big Band Leader	Recording Info
Chameleon	Maynard Ferguson	Sony Legacy 46112
Tonight Show Band (vol. 1 & 2)	Doc Severinsen	Amherst
Long Yellow Road	Toshiko Akiyoshi	BMG/RCA (B00000GAYU)
Opening Night: Thad Jones/Mel Lewis Big Band at the Village Vanguard	Thad Jones & Mel Lewis	Alan Grand Productions #1939 (B0000640MK)
Ken Burns Jazz Collection: Count Basie	Count Basie	Polygram Records #549090
Ken Burns Jazz Collection: Duke Ellington	Duke Ellington	Sony #61444
The Essential Glen Miller	Glen Miller	RCA #66520 (B000002WRM)
Carnegie Hall Jazz Concert	Benny Goodman	Sony #65143 (B00002MZ2L)
This Is Tommy Dorsey & His Orchestra	Tommy Dorsey	Collectables #2815 (B00005B51I)
The Best of Harry James	Harry James	Curb Records #77391 (B000000CXI)
Lunceford Special: 1949–1950	Jimmy Lunceford	Sony #65647 (B00005LNAX)
Dream Band (vols. 1–5)	Terry Gibbs	Contemporary #7654 (B000000X99)
Serendipity 18	Bob Florence	Mama Foundation #1025 (B00000I4ZS)
Coming About	Maria Schneider	Enja #9069 (B000005CC5)
Latin From Manhattan	Bob Mintzer	DMP #523 (B0000064UG)
Vavoom!	Brian Setzer Orchestra	Interscope Records #490733 (B00004U8KD)

OTHER GREAT RECORDINGS WITH TRUMPET

Album Title	Artist	Style	Recording Info
The Best of Irakere	Arturo Sandoval	Latin/fusion	Columbia CK 57719
The Very Best of Tito Puente	Tito Puente, et al	Latin	BMG 74465 99001 2
Chase	Bill Chase, et al	Rock/Jazz fusion	One Way Records #26660
Blood, Sweat and Tears' Greatest Hits	Lew Soloff, et al	Rock/Jazz fusion	Sony #65729
What Is Hip: Anthology	Tower of Power	Funk	Rhino Records #75788

Album Title	Artist	Style	Recording Info
Earth, Wind and Fire: Greatest Hits	EWF	Rock/Jazz fusion	Sony #65779
Jump, Jive and Wail	Brian Setzer Orchestra	Neo-swing/Rockabilly	Interscope Records
Hot	Squirrel Nut Zippers	Neo-swing	Mammoth/PGD #980137
Big Bad Voodoo Daddy	**BBVD**	**Neo-swing**	**Interscope Records**
Zoot Suit Riot	Cherry Poppin' Daddies	Neo-swing	Mojo/Jive (B00005RIJH)
The Very Best of Kool & the Gang	Spike Michens, et al	Funk	Mercury / Universal B00000IJVE
The Best of James Brown	James Brown, et al	Funk	B00000JMKD
The Very Best of Chicago: Only the Beginning	Lee Loughane, et al	Rock	Rhino/Wea B000068ZVQ

NOTES FROM THE EDGE: AVANT GARDE

We crafty humans are always striving for the different, the new; things as yet unheard, unspoken, or unseen. It's the explorer that lurks in the blood of most humans. Music also benefits from this curious trait of ours because it is the ability to explore and experiment and innovate that brings us new styles of music.

Following are some examples of the more risky and daring endeavors involving trumpet. This is the list I'm most nervous about posting, because unless you're tuned in to this scene, it's easy to miss some new, edgy artists. If you know of any I'm leaving out (and I'm sure that's a big list), please let me know.

Album Title	Artist	General Info	Recording Info
Electric Bath	Don Ellis	Electrified 1/4-tone Trumpet	GNP Crescendo GNPD 2223
Bionic: Krunk Jazz	Russell Gunn	Crunk Jazz	CD Baby
Ethnomusicology, Vol. 1	Russell Gunn	Jazz Meets Hip-hop	Atlantic 83165-2
Constellations	Dave Douglas	Jazz-Eastern European-Classical	Hat Art CD 7165
Freak In	Dave Douglas	Jazz-Electronica	RCA (B0000894PB)
A Tribute to Jack Johnson	Miles Davis	Angry Trumpet Rock	Columbia CK 47036
Americans Swinging in Paris	Art Ensemble of Chicago	Free Jazz Masters	EMI International (B000065BS0)
This Is Our Music	Don Cherry	Free Jazz	Atlantic

WATCH AND LEARN: TRUMPETERS ON VIDEO

As if you didn't have enough to go through already, right? Well, if you can't see master trumpet players live, video is the next best thing. When we actually *see* someone playing some mad trumpet music, it makes the experience more amazing, more real. Instead of getting just the sound, with video you can actually see these masters showing their soul. It's amazing! Plus, it's a lot easier to transcribe a musical idea when you can see which valves to push.

Video Title (Artist)	Length (if available)	Produced By
Satchmo: Louis Armstrong	86 min.	CMV Enterprises
Let's Get Lost (Chet Baker)		Columbia Video
Bix: Ain't None of Them Play Like Him Yet		Playboy Home Video
Miles Ahead: the Music of Miles Davis	60 min.	WNET/13 in assoc. w/Obenhaus Films, Inc., Toby/Byron Multiprises
The Miles Davis Story	125 min.	Columbia Music Video, 2001
A Night in Tunisia: A Musical Portrait of Dizzy Gillespie	28 min.	View Video Educational Video Network, 1990
Things to Come: Dizzy Gillespie and Billy Eckstine	55 min.	Vintage Jazz Classics, 1993
Dizzy Gillespie and the United Nations Orchestra	90 min.	Eagle Eye Video
Jazz then-Dixieland, 1 & 2 (Al Hirt)	60 min.	Century Home Video, 1983
Blues & Swing (Wynton Marsalis)	79 min.	Clearvue/eav, 1988
Tackling the Monster: Marsalis on Practice (Wynton Marsalis)	53 min.	Sony Classical Film & Video, 1995
Listening for Clues: Marsalis on Form	53 min.	Sony Classical Film & Video, 1995
A Unique Approach to Improvising on Chords & Scales (John McNeil, et al)	53 min.	International Production Group, Inc., 2000
Becoming an Improviser: Creative Practice with Chords & Scales (John McNeil, Rufus Reid, et al)	56 min.	International Production Group, Inc., 2000
Spera on Jazz (Dominic Spera)	160 min.	University of Wisconsin, Madison, 1986
Trumpet Course: Beginning to Intermediate (Clark Terry)	50 min.	Kultur International Films, 1981, 1990
Steps to Excellence: A Trumpet Clinic (Allen Vizzutti)		Yamaha Musical Products, 1984
One Night With Blue Note		Blue Note Records, 2003

LISTEN TO OTHER ARTISTS

Here is a list of other jazz musicians to listen to: **saxophonists** Charlie Parker, Sonny Rollins, Stan Getz, Sonny Stitt, Phil Woods, Ornette Coleman, Joe Henderson, David Murray, Frank Morgan, Bobby Watson, Tim Berne, John Zorn, Chico Freeman, Courtney Pine, Joe Lovano, Bob Berg, and Jerry Bergonzi; **clarinetists** Benny Goodman, Artie Shaw, Don Byron, and Eddie Daniels; **trombonists** Bill Watrous, Steve Turre, Robin Eubanks, and Ray Anderson; **pianists** Duke Ellington, Count Basie, Oscar Peterson, Thelonius Monk, Dave Brubeck, Herbie Hancock, Cecil Taylor, Geri Allen, Mulgrew Miller, Kenny Barron, Gonzalo Rubalcaba, Eduard Simon, Renee Rosnes, and Marilyn Crispell; **guitarists** Charlie Christian, Django Reinhardt, Joe Pass, Wes Montgomery, John Scofield, Bill Frisell, and Kevin Eubanks; **vibraphonists** Lionel Hampton, Steve Nelson, and Gary Burton; **bassists** Ray Brown, Christian McBride, John Clayton, Charlie Haden, Dave Holland, Niels-Henning Oersted Pedersen, and Lonnie Plaxico; **drummers** Chick Webb, Max Roach, Art Blakey, Buddy Rich, and Tony Williams, and **vocalists** Ella Fitzgerald, Billie Holliday, Sarah Vaughan, Frank Sinatra, Nina Simone, Bobby McFerrin, and Cassandra Wilson.

Here are a few classical musicians to listen to: **pianists** Glen Gould (esp. the *Goldberg Variations*), Emil Gilels (esp. Beethoven piano sonatas 21, 23, 26), Murray Perahia (also the *Goldberg Variations*), Arthur Rubinstein (Chopin ballades and scherzi), Paul Jacobs (Debusy piano preludes), Vladimir Horowitz (Carnegie Hall Concert 1965), Stephen Hough (Liszt Piano Sonata in B minor), and Van Cliburn (Tchaikovsky Piano Concerto No. 1); **string players** Yo Yo Ma (cello, esp. the *Bach Cello Suites*), Mstislav Rostropovich (cello, Dvoràk Cello Concerto in B minor), John Williams (guitar, any recording), Andres Segovia (guitar, any recording), Christopher Parkening (guitar, any recording), and the Emerson String Quartet (Beethoven string quartets); **flutists** Jean Pierre Rampal and James Galway; and keep an ear out for **conductors** Sir Georg Solti, Fritz Reiner, Kurt Masur, Michael Tilson Thomas, Leonard Bernstein, Herbert von Karajan, Lorin Maazel, and Daniel Barenboim.

Of course neither of these lists is complete, or even close. These are just a smattering of jazz and classical artists who come to mind immediately. Listen to as many musicians as you can. Listening will increase your awareness and appreciation for different styles of music.

CHAPTER 20

GEAR FOR YOUR EARS

The notes are in the horn. Find them.

—Charles Mingus (1922–1979)

What's Ahead:

- Tuners
- Metronomes
- Microphones
- Recording devices
- Cases
- Electronic effects

Terms to Know:

MM: Maelzel's Metronome, or Metronome Marking. Used to indicate tempo. MM=120 is the same as 120 beats per minute.

bpm: Beats per minute.

cent: A measurement of sound frequency. There are 100 cents in a half step.

XLR: An audio cable used to connect microphones to audio devices. It has three pins and provides balanced input.

track: A distinct selection of music from a recording.

effects pedal: A device used to shape amplified sound. The effect is turned on and off via a foot pedal.

WHY DO I NEED MORE STUFF?

Some of the items in this chapter are certainly not necessary. Keep in mind that the most important thing in this adventure of yours is making music. For that, all you need is your horn. You don't even need a case. Charlie Parker carried his alto saxophone around in a paper bag for a while. I don't recommend it.

That being said, however, there are some big benefits with some of this stuff, and some of the benefits are so incredibly helpful that you really should get the thing. I'll let you know if an item is a "must have."

Stand by Me

If you're reading music, you need a stand. In addition to being handy, a stand will help to improve your posture and breathing, both of which affect your tone, range, and endurance. Propping your music in a case or on a counter is generally a pain in the neck, literally. There are many collapsible music stands on the market, and most will easily fit in a trumpet case; or consider a sturdier stand that stays in one place. Visit your local music store.

Metronome: Your Rhythmic Best Friend

This is the first gadget you absolutely must have. This tool is crucial if you want rock-solid rhythm (you *should* want this!). The metronome will not only help you stay steady, but will also be a useful tool in achieving the fastest possible tempos for your exercises or performance pieces.

Get one and use it early and often. You won't regret it. There are a bewildering number of varieties. Below are pictures of the two that I own. Go to your local music store and try out a few to see what you like. Look for a metronome with a headphone jack. Trumpet is loud enough to drown out the click.

> MM=120 means you set your metronome to 120 and it will click merrily away at 120 *beats per minute (bpm)*. The MM stands for Mazel's Metronome, or Metronome Marking.

Pendulum Metronome: Metronomes don't get any more low tech than this, and if you don't want to buy and throw away batteries, or read a user's manual, this is the metronome for you. A weight slides up and down the moving arm: the higher the weight, the slower the tempo. Metronome markings are read just above the weight position. Simple and easy to use. Just wind it up, set your tempo and go. The only downside is that this type of metronome is pretty quiet and the sound of your horn may drown it out. Here's a picture of the Taktell Mini I use when playing acoustic guitar.

Metronome/tuner (Sabine MT 9000): This is handy because it's both a metronome *and* a tuner. It will subdivide the beat in many different patterns from sixteenth notes to swing eighth notes, will click in meters up to seven beats long, has an analog arm that sweeps back and forth, has volume control, and has an earphone jack. The tuner can be calibrated and its analog arm shows pitch level in 5-cent increments. It also has a jack for guitar if you're so inclined. I've used this one for about five years with no trouble. ($30)

MICROPHONES

Trumpet is one of the loudest acoustic instruments on the planet and many performance situations won't require you to make your horn even louder. However, if you're playing for large audiences, in a loud band, or are playing with a harmon mute and need more volume, you'll want a microphone (mic) and something to amplify the sound. In addition, if you plan to record yourself for any reason, a microphone of some sort is a must. There are two basic types of microphones: condenser mics and dynamic mics.

Dynamic Microphones

Dynamic mics don't need a power source. The vibrations of the source (your horn) are sensed by the mic and the vibrations are turned into a signal that is sent to the soundboard or the amplifier.

Shure SM58: This mic is known for its ability to withstand abuse that would ruin most other microphones. I own one because it's inexpensive and sturdy and it reproduces my trumpet sound with pretty good accuracy. The price is a bargain considering its life expectancy. ($100)

Condenser Microphones

Condenser mics *do* need a power source. This usually is supplied by batteries, or phantom power, a power source sent through the cord to the mic. A tiny diaphragm within the mic vibrates when sound waves are present. Because the diaphragm is powered, it reacts with much more sensitivity to sound.

Shure SM57: This is one of the most popular instrument/vocal mics because it's reliable and natural sounding. I own one and have found it pretty durable as well. It has a wide frequency response (40Hz–15kHz) which helps reproduce your trumpet tone accurately. It's ideal for up-close amplification, like when you play with a Harmon mute. ($70)

Clip-on and Wireless Microphones

The above microphones will require a stand and cords. Here are a couple alternatives that do away with the microphone stand and cords as well.

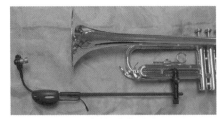

LCM-77: This is the microphone developed in association with Miles Davis and allows space between the bell and the mic so you can fit a mute in the horn easily. This mic is used and endorsed by trumpeter Chris Botti, who, in addition to his own recordings, performs and records with Sting.

Applied Microphone Technology Roam 1: If you want to do without wires altogether, this is a great option. Not only is it wireless, but the mic is in a shock mount to avoid the noise you make when pounding down your valves. As you can see, there's still room for a mute. ($580)

RECORDING DEVICES

One of the best ways to improve *all* aspects of your playing is to record and listen to yourself. The recording machine tells no lies. You have many options for recording devices and there are advantages and disadvantages to each. One of the cheapest ways is to record on a cassette tape. Tape recorders and tapes are pretty easy to find and are cheap, but it's often difficult to find your place on a cassette and the quality isn't all that great. There are much better options, and one of them is free!

Your Computer: Many computers have recording capabilities, but the quality is usually low. In my opinion the *very best* option for recording (and the most inexpensive way) is to download the free program *Audacity*. With this program you can manipulate sound in many, many ways including mixing, editing, and converting to several formats including MP3. This is a powerful program that can be used for things other than recording. For instance, you can take a piece that is very fast and slow it down without changing the pitch. Or, if a piece is too high, you can make it lower so you can play along. It's truly a great program and if you're serious about music and own a computer, you should have it. Go to http://audacity.sourceforge.net/.

Sony HI MD (mini-disc recorder): This amazingly tiny device (it's about 4 inches square) will hold up to 45 hours of recorded music as well as pictures and text and it's also a radio receiver. Its battery can last up to 14 hours. These are great little portable devices and I often use mine with students or at a gig. I'll never go back to a tape recorder. The greatest thing about this device is that you can advance to a track quickly and easily. ($250)

Korg Pandora PXR4 (multi-track recorder): But why stop there? For another fifty bucks you can get a device that will allow you to record multiple tracks. This means you can record the first trumpet part of a quartet, then go back and do the second, third, and fourth parts as well. Put it all together, hit play, and you're playing a quartet with yourself. These are also great for writing songs and figuring out harmony parts. There is also a function which lets you slow down a recording so you can learn a particularly tricky or fast lick from a tune you're trying to transcribe. A fun little device that will entertain you for hours and hours. I absolutely *love* playing with mine and also use it with my students. ($300)

CASES

There are a whole lot of ways to put dings in your horn and almost as many ways to protect it. Here are some of your case options. If your horn didn't come with a case, you'll probably want one. If you aren't satisfied with the case you have because it's too heavy, too small, or not cool enough, here are some options for you.

The Torpedo Bag: This case will withstand 400 pounds of pressure and can be worn like a backpack. Its design makes it low profile and easy to store in the overhead compartment of an airplane or just about anywhere else. Also available is a bag for mutes, or a music pouch, both of which will strap to the case and are easily detachable. This is a great little case that is very sturdy. I've been using one for several years. ($160)

Reunion Blues Gig Bag: An excellent, sturdy gig bag made of leather with a shoulder strap and outer pocket for accessories. I used one of these for many years until I bought another horn that wouldn't fit the bag. An excellent case. ($125)

Cases for more than one horn: There are quite a few multiple-horn cases out there and they can be useful if you own a flugelhorn, or C, D, and E♭ trumpets. Lugging one case to a gig instead of three (or even two) is worth the price. Run a search online to see what's available.

CHAPTER 21
FULL-LENGTH TUNES

True creativity often starts where language ends.

—Arthur Koestler (1905–1983)

Terms to Know:

improvisation: A performance given spontaneously. The musical improviser listens and plays along within certain guidelines, which may also be ignored.

plunger: A sink plunger used as a mute. Lends a vocal-like quality to the sound.

"ALL BLUES"

This is a classic jazz tune written by Miles Davis, first appearing on the incredible 1959 album *Kind of Blue*. "All Blues" has been played by musicians all over the world. It's a 12-bar-blues form, and to get the right sound you'll need a Harmon mute without the stem. The notation is shown in lead sheet style, as discussed in chapter 9. After stating the melody (or *head*) twice, it's time to improvise. You can play along with me or Sèan during our solos. I've also included the saxophone harmony part for you to play with if you like. Visit www.sol-ut.com for more resources to help you with this.

All Blues

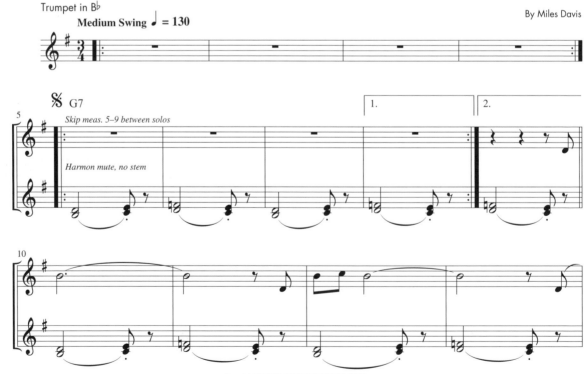

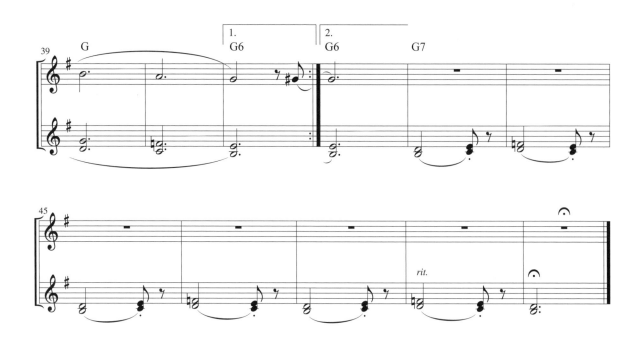

"ELEANOR RIGBY"

This classic Beatles tune first appeared on the 1966 album *Revolver* and has since been covered by bands in many, many styles. Listen to the original if you don't know it. Here is another version.

Eleanor Rigby

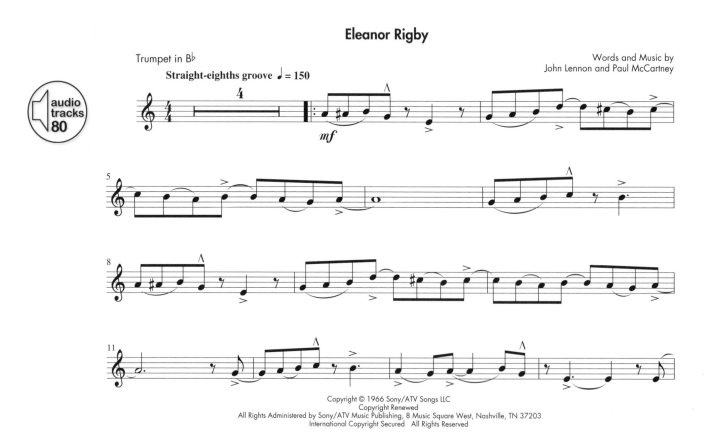

Words and Music by
John Lennon and Paul McCartney

"I WAN'NA BE LIKE YOU"

The Disney movie *The Jungle Book* had some great tunes in it. Trumpeter and entertainer Louis Prima did the voice of King Louis in the movie, and also played the trumpet solo in this tune, so it seemed like a natural choice. I arranged it to be low in the trumpet range and fun to play. The basic melody is shown on the next page, but you'll notice that many rhythmic nuances are played on the CD version. Use a plunger mute for extra vocal-like sounds. You get to improvise again in the middle of this tune. Visit sol-ut.com for tips and solo ideas as well as other supplemental material to practice.

I Wan'na Be Like You (The Monkey Song)
from Walt Disney's THE JUNGLE BOOK

Words and Music by
Richard M. Sherman and Robert B. Sherman

"OYE COMO VA"

This tune by timbalero Tito Puente first appeared on his 1962 album entitled *El Rey Bravo* (the brave king), and was a huge hit for Carlos Santana. It appeared on his 1970 album *Abraxas*. This is a short and simple version which you should have fun with.

Oye Como Va

Trumpet in B♭

Words and Music by Tito Puente

"WELL, YOU NEEDN'T"

Another jazz classic by Thelonius Monk. Though many musicians have covered this tune, it is Miles Davis's version from the great album *Steamin'* that most are familiar with. I've arranged the tune as a lead sheet to be a little easier to improvise over. There is an intro and then a *vamp* (repeated passage) after the first time through the form (AABA). Improvising tips can be found at sol-ut.com. The range on this can be challenging, as is the fingerwork in the middle section. Keep your air moving and practice slowly.

APPENDIX

TRACK LIST

Chapter 2: What the Buzz Is All About

1. lip buzz
2. long buzz
3. start and stop buzz
4. high to low buzz
5. high-low-middle buzz
6. see-saw buzz
7. pitch-matching buzz
8. descending/ascending chromatic scale buzz

Chapter 5: The Practice of Practice

9. warm-up buzz
10. tongue warm-up
11. chromatic warm-up 1
12. chromatic warm-up 2

Chapter 6: Reading and Writing, But No 'rithmetic

13. C and G
14. D, E, and F
15. C major example 1
16. C major example 2
17. changing notes
18. skipping notes
19. low notes
20. high notes

Chapter 7: Tongue Tips for Trumpet

21. buzz tonguing
22. horn tonguing
23. syllable tonguing
24. double-tonguing 1
25. double-tonguing 2
26. "Scheherazade"
27. triple-tonguing buzz
28. triple-tonguing horn
29. multiple tonguing 1
30. multiple tonguing 2
31. multiple tonguing 3
32. multiple tonguing 4
33. multiple tonguing 5
34. multiple tonguing 6
35. multiple tonguing 7

Chapter 8: Lip Slurs and the Oral Cavity

36. slur 1
37. slur 2
38. slur 3
39. slur 4
40. slur 5
41. slur 6

Chapter 9: Tunes from Simple to Sophisticated

42. "Mary Had a Little Lamb"
43. "Au Clair De La Lune"
44. "Twinkle, Twinkle Little Star"
45. "Jingle Bells"
46. eighth notes
47. "Hot Cross Buns"
48. "Skip to My Lou"
49. "Leonore Overture No. 3"
50. "Theme–Pictures at an Exhibition"
51. "Trumpet Concerto in E♭ Major"
52. "Carnival of Venice"
53. "Symphony 5, Movement 1"
54. "Ride of the Valkyries"
55. "Fêtes"
56. "Also Sprach Zarathustra"
57. "Trumpet Shall Sound"
58. "Magnificat"
59. "Dark Eyes"

Chapter 11: How Low Can You Go? Pedal Tones

60. pedal exercise 1
61. pedal exercise 2

Chapter 12: Home on the High Range

62. loose lip flap

Chapter 15: Trumpet Sound Effects

63. vibrato
64. alternate fingerings
65. scoop
66. doit
67. rip
68. fall

69. whinny
70. growl
71. flutter
72. trill
73. mordent
74. turn
75. grace
76. appoggiatura
77. shake

Chapter 16: Mutes, Dampfers, and Plungers, Oh My!

78. plunger

Chapter 21: Full-Length Tunes

79. "All Blues," by Miles Davis
80. "Eleanor Rigby," by the Beatles
81. "I Wan'na Be Like You," (the Monkey Song from Disney's *Jungle Book*)
82. "Oye Como Va," by Tito Puente
83. "Well, You Needn't," by Thelonious Monk

TRUMPET FINGERING CHART

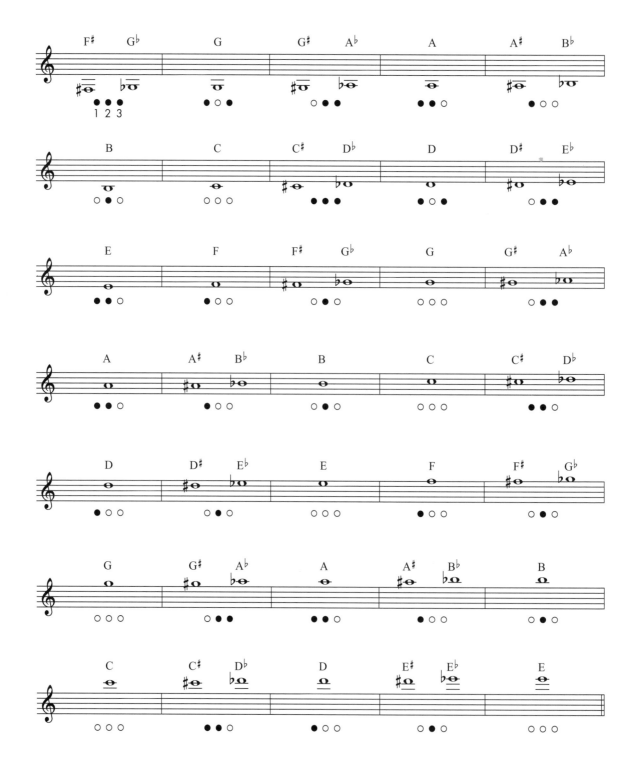

ALTERNATE TRUMPET FINGERINGS

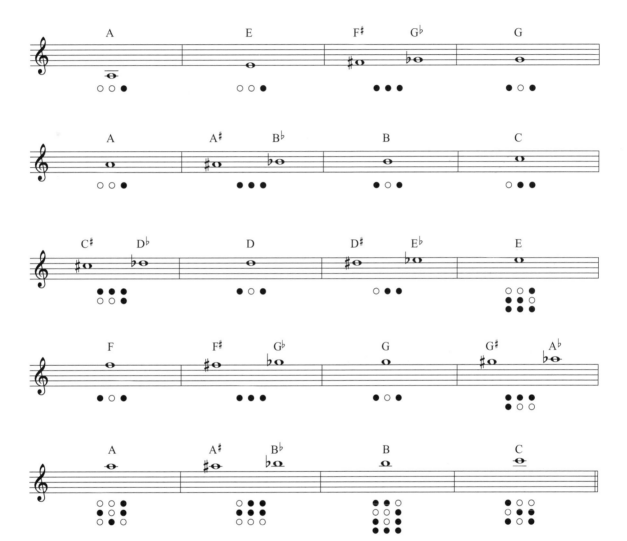

Presenting the Hal Leonard JAZZ PLAY ALONG SERIES

DUKE ELLINGTON Vol. 1
Caravan • Don't Get Around Much Anymore • In a Sentimental Mood • Perdido • Prelude to a Kiss • Satin Doll • Take the "A" Train • and more.
00841644 ....$16.95

MILES DAVIS Vol. 2
All Blues • Blue in Green • Four • Half Nelson • Milestones • Nardis • Seven Steps to Heaven • So What • Solar • Tune Up.
00841645 ....$16.95

THE BLUES Vol. 3
Billie's Bounce • Birk's Works • C-Jam Blues • Freddie Freeloader • Mr. P.C. • Tenor Madness • Things Ain't What They Used to Be • and more.
00841646 ....$15.95

JAZZ BALLADS Vol. 4
Body and Soul • Here's That Rainy Day • Misty • My Funny Valentine • The Nearness of You • Polka Dots and Moonbeams • and more.
00841691 ....$15.95

BEST OF BEBOP Vol. 5
Anthropology • Donna Lee • Doxy • Epistrophy • Lady Bird • Oleo • Ornithology • Scrapple from the Apple • Woodyn' You • Yardbird Suite.
00841689 ....$15.95

JAZZ CLASSICS WITH EASY CHANGES Vol. 6
Blue Train • Comin' Home Baby • Footprints • Impressions • Killer Joe • St. Thomas • Well You Needn't • and more.
00841690 ....$15.95

ESSENTIAL JAZZ STANDARDS Vol. 7
Autumn Leaves • Lullaby of Birdland • Stella by Starlight • There Will Never Be Another You • When Sunny Gets Blue • and more.
00843000 ....$15.95

ANTONIO CARLOS JOBIM AND THE ART OF THE BOSSA NOVA Vol. 8
The Girl from Ipanema • How Insensitive • Meditation • One Note Samba • Quiet Nights of Quiet Stars • Slightly Out of Tune • and more.
00843001 ....$16.95

DIZZY GILLESPIE Vol. 9
Birk's Works • Con Alma • Groovin' High • Manteca • A Night in Tunisia • Salt Peanuts • Tour De Force • Woodyn' You • and more.
00843002 ....$15.95

DISNEY CLASSICS Vol. 10
Alice in Wonderland • Cruella De Vil • When You Wish upon a Star • You've Got a Friend in Me • Zip-a-Dee-Doo-Dah • and more.
00843003 ....$15.95

RODGERS AND HART FAVORITES Vol. 11
Bewitched • Dancing on the Ceiling • Have You Met Miss Jones? • I Could Write a Book • The Lady Is a Tramp • My Romance • and more.
00843004 ....$15.95

ESSENTIAL JAZZ CLASSICS Vol. 12
Airegin • Ceora • The Frim Fram Sauce • Israel • Milestones • Nefertiti • Red Clay • Satin Doll • Song for My Father • Take Five.
00843005 ....$15.95

JOHN COLTRANE Vol. 13
Blue Train • Countdown • Cousin Mary • Equinox • Giant Steps • Impressions • Lazy Bird • Mr. P.C. • Moment's Notice • Naima.
00843006 ....$16.95

IRVING BERLIN Vol. 14
Blue Skies • How Deep Is the Ocean • I've Got My Love to Keep Me Warm • Steppin' Out with My Baby • What'll I Do? • and more.
00843007 ....$14.95

RODGERS & HAMMERSTEIN Vol. 15
Do I Love You Because You're Beautiful? • It Might as Well Be Spring • My Favorite Things • Younger than Springtime • and more.
00843008 ....$14.95

COLE PORTER Vol. 16
Easy to Love • I Concentrate on You • I've Got You Under My Skin • It's All Right with Me • It's De-Lovely • You'd Be So Nice to Come Home To • and more.
00843009 ....$15.95

COUNT BASIE Vol. 17
All of Me • April in Paris • Blues in Hoss Flat • Li'l Darlin' • Moten Swing • One O'Clock Jump • Shiny Stockings • Until I Met You • and more.
00843010 ....$16.95

HAROLD ARLEN Vol. 18
Ac-cent-tchu-ate the Positive • Come Rain or Come Shine • I've Got the World on a String • Stormy Weather • That Old Black Magic • and more.
00843011 ....$16.95

COOL JAZZ Vol. 19
Bernie's Tune • Boplicity • Budo • Conception • Django • Five Brothers • Line for Lyons • Walkin' Shoes • Waltz for Debby • Whisper Not.
00843012 ....$15.95

CHRISTMAS CAROLS Vol. 20
Away in a Manger • Greensleeves • Hark! the Herald Angels Sing • Joy to the World • O Little Town of Bethlehem • Silent Night • more.
00843080 ....$14.95

RODGERS AND HART CLASSICS Vol. 21
Falling in Love with Love • Isn't it Romantic? • Manhattan • My Funny Valentine • This Can't Be Love • Thou Swell • Where or When • and more.
00843014 ....$14.95

WAYNE SHORTER Vol. 22
Children of the Night • ESP • Footprints • Juju • Mahjong • Nefertiti • Nightdreamer • Speak No Evil • Witch Hunt • Yes and No.
00843015 ....$16.95

LATIN JAZZ Vol. 23
Agua De Beber • Chega De Saudade • Manha De Carnaval • Mas Que Nada • Ran Kan Kan • So Nice • Watch What Happens • and more.
00843016 ....$16.95

EARLY JAZZ STANDARDS Vol. 24
After You've Gone • Avalon • Indian Summer • Indiana • Ja-Da • Limehouse Blues • Paper Doll • Poor Butterfly • Rose Room • St. Louis Blues.
00843017 ....$14.95

CHRISTMAS JAZZ Vol. 25
The Christmas Song (Chestnuts Roasting on an Open Fire) • I'll Be Home for Christmas • Let It Snow! Let It Snow! Let It Snow! • Silver Bells • and more.
00843018 ....$16.95

CHARLIE PARKER Vol. 26
Au Privave • Billie's Bounce • Donna Lee • My Little Suede Shoes • Ornithology • Scrapple from the Apple • Yardbird Suite • and more.
00843019 ....$16.95

GREAT JAZZ STANDARDS Vol. 27
Fly Me to the Moon • How High the Moon • I Can't Get Started with You • Speak Low • Tangerine • Willow Weep for Me • and more.
00843020 ....$14.95

BIG BAND ERA Vol. 28
Air Mail Special • Christopher Columbus • In the Mood • Jersey Bounce • Opus One • Stompin' at the Savoy • Tuxedo Junction • and more.
00843021 ....$14.95

LENNON AND McCARTNEY Vol. 29
And I Love Her • Blackbird • Come Together • Eleanor Rigby • Let It Be • Ticket to Ride • Yesterday • and more.
00843022 ....$16.95

BLUES' BEST Vol. 30
Basin Street Blues • Bloomdido • Happy Go Lucky Local • K.C. Blues • Sonnymoon for Two • Take the Coltrane • Turnaround • Twisted • and more.
00843023 ....$14.95

JAZZ IN THREE Vol. 31
Bluesette • Jitterbug Waltz • Moon River • Tennessee Waltz • West Coast Blues • What the World Needs Now Is Love • Wives and Lovers • and more.
00843024 ....$14.95

BEST OF SWING Vol. 32
Alright, Okay, You Win • Cherokee • I'll Be Seeing You • Jump, Jive an' Wail • On the Sunny Side of the Street • Route 66 • Sentimental Journey • and more.
00843025 ....$14.95

SONNY ROLLINS Vol. 33
Airegin • Alfie's Theme • Biji • The Bridge • Doxy • First Moves • Here's to the People • Oleo • St. Thomas • Sonnymoon for Two.
00843029 ....$15.95

ALL TIME STANDARDS Vol. 34
Autumn in New York • Bye Bye Blackbird • Call Me Irresponsible • Georgia on My Mind • Honeysuckle Rose • Stardust • The Very Thought of You • more.
00843030 ....$14.95

BLUESY JAZZ Vol. 35
Angel Eyes • Bags' Groove • Bessie's Blues • Chitlins Con Carne • Mercy, Mercy, Mercy • Night Train • Sweet Georgia Bright • and more.
00843031 ....$14.95

HORACE SILVER Vol. 36
Doodlin' • The Jody Grind • Nica's Dream • Opus De Funk • Peace • The Preacher • Senor Blues • Sister Sadie • Song for My Father • Strollin'.
00843032 ....$15.95

BILL EVANS Vol. 37
Funkallero • My Bells • One for Helen • The Opener • Orbit • Show-Type Tune • 34 Skidoo • Time Remembered • Turn Out the Stars • Waltz for Debby.
00843033 ....$16.95

YULETIDE JAZZ Vol. 38
Blue Christmas • Christmas Time Is Here • Merry Christmas, Darling • The Most Wonderful Time of the Year • Santa Claus Is Comin' to Town • and more.
00843034 ....$15.95

"ALL THE THINGS YOU ARE" & MORE JEROME KERN SONGS Vol. 39
All the Things You Are • Can't Help Lovin' Dat Man • A Fine Romance • Long Ago (And Far Away) • The Way You Look Tonight • Yesterdays • and more.
00843035 ....$14.95

OSSA NOVA Vol. 40

lack Orpheus • Call Me • A Man and a Woman • nly Trust Your Heart • The Shadow of Your Smile Watch What Happens • Wave • and more.
0843036 ....$14.95

LASSIC DUKE ELLINGTON Vol. 41

otton Tail • Do Nothin' Till You Hear from Me • Got It Bad and That Ain't Good • I'm Beginning See the Light • Mood Indigo • Solitude • nd more.
0843037 ....$15.95

ERRY MULLIGAN FAVORITES Vol. 42

ark for Barksdale • Dragonfly • Elevation • Idol ossip • Jeru • The Lonely Night (Night Lights) • oblesse • Rock Salt a/k/a Rocker • Theme for bim • Wallflower.
0843038 ....$15.95

ERRY MULLIGAN CLASSICS Vol. 43

pple Core • Line for Lyons • Nights at the rntable • Song for Strayhorn • Walkin' Shoes • nd more.
0843039 ....$16.95

LIVER NELSON Vol. 44

he Drive • Emancipation Blues • Hoe-Down • I emember Bird • Miss Fine • Stolen Moments • raight Ahead • Teenie's Blues • Yearnin'.
0843040 ....$16.95

AZZ AT THE MOVIES Vol. 45

aby Elephant Walk • God Bless' the Child • The ook of Love • The Rainbow Connection • winging on a Star • Thanks for the Memory • nd more.
0843041 ....$14.95

ROADWAY JAZZ STANDARDS Vol. 46

in't Misbehavin' • I've Grown Accustomed to er Face • Make Someone Happy • Old Devil oon • Small World • Till There Was You • and ore.
0843042 ....$14.95

LASSIC JAZZ BALLADS Vol. 47

lame It on My Youth • It's Easy to Remember • ne in January • Love Letters • A Nightingale ng in Berkeley Square • When I Fall in Love • nd more.
0843043 ....$14.95

EBOP CLASSICS Vol. 48

e-Bop • Bird Feathers • Blue 'N Boogie • Byrd ke • Cool Blues • Dance of the Indifels • exterity • Dizzy Atmosphere • Groovin' High • mpus Fugit.
0843044 ....$15.95

IILES DAVIS STANDARDS Vol. 49

arn That Dream • I Loves You, Porgy • If I Were Bell • On Green Dolphin Street • Some Day My rince Will Come • Yesterdays • and more.
0843045 ....$16.95

GREAT JAZZ CLASSICS Vol. 50

Along Came Betty • The Jive Samba • Little Sunflower • Nuages • Peri's Scope • Phase Dance • Road Song • Think on Me • Windows.
00843046 ....$14.95

UP-TEMPO JAZZ Vol. 51

Cherokee (Indian Love Song) • Chi Chi • 52nd Street Theme • Little Willie Leaps • Move • Pent Up House • Topsy • and more.
00843047 ....$14.95

STEVIE WONDER Vol. 52

I Just Called to Say I Love You • Isn't She Lovely • My Cherie Amour • Part Time Lover • Superstition • You Are the Sunshine of My Life • and more.
00843048 ....$15.95

RHYTHM CHANGES Vol. 53

Celia • Chasing the Bird • Cotton Tail • Crazeology • Fox Hunt • I Got Rhythm • No Moe • Oleo • Red Cross • Steeplechase.
00843049 ....$14.95

"MOONLIGHT IN VERMONT" AND OTHER GREAT STANDARDS Vol. 54

A Child Is Born • Love You Madly • Lover Man (Oh, Where Can You Be?) • Moonlight in Vermont • The Night Has a Thousand Eyes • Small Fry • and more.
00843050 ....$14.95

BENNY GOLSON Vol. 55

Along Came Betty • Blues March • Gypsy Jingle-Jangle • I Remember Clifford • Killer Joe • Step Lightly • Whisper Not • and more.
00843052 ....$15.95

VINCE GUARALDI Vol. 57

Blue Charlie Brown • Christmas Time Is Here • Frieda (With the Naturally Curly Hair) • The Great Pumpkin Waltz • Happiness Theme • Linus and Lucy • Oh, Good Grief • The Pebble Beach Theme • Skating • Surfin' Snoopy.
00843057 ....$15.95

MORE LENNON AND McCARTNEY Vol. 58

Can't Buy Me Love • Michelle • Norwegian Wood (This Bird Has Flown) • Eight Days a Week • Yellow Submarine • In My Life • The Long and Winding Road • All My Loving • Julia • Ob-La-Di, Ob-La-Da.
00843059 ....$14.95

SOUL JAZZ Vol. 59

The Cape Verdean Blues • Cold Duck Time • Dat Dere • Freight Trane • Holy Land • The Jive Samba • Nutville • Unit Seven • Work Song.
00843060 ....$14.95

MONGO SANTAMARIA Vol. 61

Afro Blue • Come Candela • Federico • Las Guajiras • Linda Guajira • Manila • Sabroso • Watermelon Man.
00843062 ....$15.95

JAZZ-ROCK FUSION Vol. 62

Brown Hornet • Chameleon • Got a Match? • Loose Ends • Revelation • Snakes • Spain • Three Views of a Secret • Watermelon Man.
00843063 ....$14.95

CLASSICAL JAZZ Vol. 63

Eine Kleine Nachtmusik • Emperor Waltz • Habanera • Jesu, Joy of Man's Desiring • Minuet in G • New World Symphony (Theme) • Nocturne in F Minor • Ode to Joy • Pavane • Pavane (For a Dead Princess).
00843064 ....$14.95

TV TUNES Vol. 64

Bandstand Boogie • Theme from Family Guy • Theme from Frasier • Hawaii Five-O Theme • Love and Marriage • Mission: Impossible Theme • The Odd Couple • Theme from the Simpsons • Theme from Spider Man • Theme from Star Trek®.
00843065 ....$14.95

SMOOTH JAZZ Vol. 65

Angela • Cast Your Fate to the Wind • Feels So Good • Give Me the Night • Just the Two of Us • Minute by Minute • Morning Dance • Songbird • Street Life • This Masquerade.
00843066 ....$14.95

A CHARLIE BROWN CHRISTMAS Vol. 66

Christmas Is Coming • The Christmas Song (Chestnuts Roasting on an Open Fire) • Christmas Time Is Here • Linus and Lucy • My Little Drum • O Tannenbaum • Skating • What Child Is This.
00843067 ....$15.95

CHICK COREA Vol. 67

Bud Powell • Captain Marvel • 500 Miles High • Litha • The Loop • Mirror, Mirror • Now He Beats the Drum, Now He Stops • (I Can Recall) Spain • Tones for Joan's Bones • Windows.
00843068 ....$15.95

CHARLES MINGUS Vol. 68

Better Get Hit in Your Soul • Boogie Stop Shuffle • Goodbye Pork Pie Hat • Gunslinging Bird • Jelly Roll • Nostalgia in Times Square • Peggy's Blue Skylight • Pithecanthropus Erectus • Portrait • Slippers.
00843069 ....$16.95

CLASSIC JAZZ Vol. 69

Allen's Alley • Detour Ahead • I Wished on the Moon • Let's Get Lost • Nobody Else but Me • Our Delight • Rockin' in Rhythm • A Sleepin' Bee • Soul Eyes • What Is There to Say.
00843071 ....$14.95

THE DOORS Vol. 70

Break on Through to the Other Side • The End • Hello, I Love You (Won't You Tell Me Your Name?) • L.A. Woman • Light My Fire • Love Me Two Times • People Are Strange • Riders on the Storm • Roadhouse Blues • Touch Me.
00843072 ....$14.95

COLE PORTER CLASSICS Vol. 71

Dream Dancing • From This Moment On • I Get a Kick out of You • I Love Paris • I've Got My Eyes on You • Just One of Those Things • Love for Sale • My Heart Belongs to Daddy • Night and Day • What Is This Thing Called Love?
00843073 ....$14.95

CLASSIC JAZZ BALLADS Vol. 72

For Heaven's Sake • Isfahan • Lament • Maybe You'll Be There • The Single Petal of a Rose • Some Other Spring • Sure Thing • Too Young to Go Steady • You're Looking at Me • You've Changed.
00843074 ....$14.95

JAZZ/BLUES Vol. 73

Break Out the Blues • Bremond's Blues • Gee Baby, Ain't I Good to You • I'll Close My Eyes • Movin' Along (Sid's Twelve) • Night Lights • Reunion Blues • The Sermon • Sunny • This Here.
00843075 ....$14.95

0108

ARTIST TRANSCRIPTIONS®

3 1125 00721 2309

Artist Transcriptions are authentic, note-for-note transcriptions of today's hottest artists in jazz, pop and rock. These outstanding, accurate arrangements are in an easy-to-read format which includes all essential lines. Artist Transcriptions can be used to perform, sequence or for reference.

CLARINET

00672423	Buddy De Franco Collection	$19.95

FLUTE

00672379	Eric Dolphy Collection	$19.95
00672372	James Moody Collection – Sax and Flute	$19.95
00660108	James Newton – Improvising Flute	$14.95
00672455	Lew Tabackin Collection	$19.95

GUITAR & BASS

00660113	The Guitar Style of George Benson	$14.95
00672331	Ron Carter – Acoustic Bass	$16.95
00660115	Al Di Meola – Friday Night in San Francisco	$14.95
00604043	Al Di Meola – Music, Words, Pictures	$14.95
00673245	Jazz Style of Tal Farlow	$19.95
00672359	Bela Fleck and the Flecktones	$18.95
00699389	Jim Hall – Jazz Guitar Environments	$19.95
00699306	Jim Hall – Exploring Jazz Guitar	$19.95
00672335	Best of Scott Henderson	$24.95
00672356	Jazz Guitar Standards	$19.95
00675536	Wes Montgomery – Guitar Transcriptions	$17.95
00672353	Joe Pass Collection	$18.95
00673216	John Patitucci	$16.95
00672374	Johnny Smith Guitar Solos	$16.95
00672320	Mark Whitfield	$19.95
00672337	Gary Willis Collection	$19.95

PIANO & KEYBOARD

00672338	Monty Alexander Collection	$19.95
00672487	Monty Alexander Plays Standards	$19.95
00672318	Kenny Barron Collection	$22.95
00672520	Count Basie Collection	$19.95
00672364	Warren Bernhardt Collection	$19.95
00672439	Cyrus Chestnut Collection	$19.95
00673242	Billy Childs Collection	$19.95
00672300	Chick Corea – Paint the World	$12.95
00672537	Bill Evans at Town Hall	$16.95
00672425	Bill Evans – Piano Interpretations	$19.95
00672365	Bill Evans – Piano Standards	$19.95
00672510	Bill Evans Trio – Vol. 1: 1959-1961	$24.95
00672511	Bill Evans Trio – Vol. 2: 1962-1965	$24.95
00672512	Bill Evans Trio – Vol. 3: 1968-1974	$24.95
00672513	Bill Evans Trio – Vol. 4: 1979-1980	$24.95
00672329	Benny Green Collection	$19.95
00672486	Vince Guaraldi Collection	$19.95
00672419	Herbie Hancock Collection	$19.95
00672446	Gene Harris Collection	$19.95
00672438	Hampton Hawes	$19.95
00672322	Ahmad Jamal Collection	$22.95
00672476	Brad Mehldau Collection	$19.95

00672390	Thelonious Monk Plays Jazz Standards – Volume 1	$19.95
00672391	Thelonious Monk Plays Jazz Standards – Volume 2	$19.95
00672433	Jelly Roll Morton – The Piano Rolls	$12.95
00672542	Oscar Peterson – Jazz Piano Solos	$14.95
00672544	Oscar Peterson – Originals	$9.95
00672532	Oscar Peterson – Plays Broadway	$19.95
00672531	Oscar Peterson – Plays Duke Ellington	$19.95
00672533	Oscar Peterson – Trios	$24.95
00672543	Oscar Peterson Trio – Canadiana Suite	$7.95
00672534	Very Best of Oscar Peterson	$22.95
00672371	Bud Powell Classics	$19.95
00672376	Bud Powell Collection	$19.95
00672437	André Previn Collection	$19.95
00672507	Gonzalo Rubalcaba Collection	$19.95
00672303	Horace Silver Collection	$19.95
00672316	Art Tatum Collection	$22.95
00672355	Art Tatum Solo Book	$19.95
00672357	Billy Taylor Collection	$24.95
00673215	McCoy Tyner	$16.95
00672321	Cedar Walton Collection	$19.95
00672519	Kenny Werner Collection	$19.95
00672434	Teddy Wilson Collection	$19.95

SAXOPHONE

00673244	Julian "Cannonball" Adderley Collection	$19.95
00673237	Michael Brecker	$19.95
00672429	Michael Brecker Collection	$19.95
00672351	Brecker Brothers... And All Their Jazz	$19.95
00672447	Best of the Brecker Brothers	$19.95
00672315	Benny Carter Plays Standards	$22.95
00672314	Benny Carter Collection	$22.95
00672394	James Carter Collection	$19.95
00672349	John Coltrane Plays Giant Steps	$19.95
00672529	John Coltrane – Giant Steps	$14.95
00672494	John Coltrane – A Love Supreme	$14.95
00672493	John Coltrane Plays "Coltrane Changes"	$19.95
00672453	John Coltrane Plays Standards	$19.95
00673233	John Coltrane Solos	$22.95
00672328	Paul Desmond Collection	$19.95
00672454	Paul Desmond – Standard Time	$19.95
00672379	Eric Dolphy Collection	$19.95
00672530	Kenny Garrett Collection	$19.95
00699375	Stan Getz	$18.95
00672377	Stan Getz – Bossa Novas	$19.95
00672375	Stan Getz – Standards	$17.95
00673254	Great Tenor Sax Solos	$18.95
00672523	Coleman Hawkins Collection	$19.95
00673252	Joe Henderson – Selections from "Lush Life" & "So Near So Far"	$19.95
00672330	Best of Joe Henderson	$22.95

00673239	Best of Kenny G	$19.95
00673229	Kenny G – Breathless	$19.95
00672462	Kenny G – Classics in the Key of G	$19.95
00672485	Kenny G – Faith: A Holiday Album	$14.95
00672373	Kenny G – The Moment	$19.95
00672516	Kenny G – Paradise	$14.95
00672326	Joe Lovano Collection	$19.95
00672498	Jackie McLean Collection	$19.95
00672372	James Moody Collection – Sax and Flute	$19.95
00672416	Frank Morgan Collection	$19.95
00672539	Gerry Mulligan Collection	$19.95
00672352	Charlie Parker Collection	$19.95
00672444	Sonny Rollins Collection	$19.95
00675000	David Sanborn Collection	$16.95
00672528	Bud Shank Collection	$19.95
00672491	New Best of Wayne Shorter	$19.95
00672455	Lew Tabackin Collection	$19.95
00672334	Stanley Turrentine Collection	$19.95
00672524	Lester Young Collection	$19.95

TROMBONE

00672332	J.J. Johnson Collection	$19.95
00672489	Steve Turré Collection	$19.95

TRUMPET

00672480	Louis Armstrong Collection	$14.95
00672481	Louis Armstrong Plays Standards	$14.95
00672435	Chet Baker Collection	$19.95
00673234	Randy Brecker	$17.95
00672351	Brecker Brothers... And All Their Jazz	$19.95
00672447	Best of the Brecker Brothers	$19.95
00672448	Miles Davis – Originals, Vol. 1	$19.95
00672451	Miles Davis – Originals, Vol. 2	$19.95
00672450	Miles Davis – Standards, Vol. 1	$19.95
00672449	Miles Davis – Standards, Vol. 2	$19.95
00672479	Dizzy Gillespie Collection	$19.95
00673214	Freddie Hubbard	$14.95
00672382	Tom Harrell – Jazz Trumpet	$19.95
00672363	Jazz Trumpet Solos	$9.95
00672506	Chuck Mangione Collection	$19.95
00672525	Arturo Sandoval – Trumpet Evolution	$19.95

FOR MORE INFORMATION, SEE YOUR LOCAL MUSIC DEALER, OR WRITE TO:

HAL•LEONARD®
CORPORATION
7777 W. BLUEMOUND RD. P.O. BOX 13819 MILWAUKEE, WI 53213

Visit our web site for a complete listing of our titles with songlists at
www.halleonard.com